The months and seasons mentioned apply to temperate regions of the northern hemisphere; for readers in other regions a table of approximate equivalents has been included on page 156.

First published in Great Britain in 1969 by
The Hamlyn Publishing Group Limited

This edition published in 1989 by
Treasure Press
Michelin House
81 Fulham Road
London SW3 6RB

ISBN 1 85051 457 7

Produced by Mandarin Offset
Printed and bound in Singapore

CONTENTS

THE USE OF SHRUBS

Shrubs and small trees form the backbone, as it were, of a garden, as far as plant material is concerned and they have an important part to play in garden design. They are more permanent than other plants and, although a few lend themselves to being moved to fit in with an alteration of plan, most of them will remain where they are planted for many years.

Many shrubs are grown for the beauty of their flowers, others for their foliage, others for their colourful or interesting fruits. Some combine all attributes. There are shrubs ranging in height from a few inches to 15–20 feet and small trees may be expected to reach 20–25 feet in time. There are evergreen kinds and deciduous, or 'leaf-losing', kinds. Most of those available for our gardens will do well on any soil, although there are some that will not grow on alkaline soils – those containing chalk or lime.

Many of the most beautiful shrubs in flower, leaf or fruit are used as single specimens in a lawn where they can be seen in isolation and realize their full potential without competition from neighbours. They may be used, with other fine shrubs, in an area devoted solely to the cultivation of shrubs and small trees, usually known as a 'shrubbery'.

Outline of shrubs illustrated right

Key:

1. Prunus
2. Sorbus
3. Lonicera
4. Forsythia
5. Laurel
6. Weigela
7. Mahonia
8. Rhododendron
9. Ericas
10. Berberis
11. Ceratostigma
12. Senecio
13. Potentilla

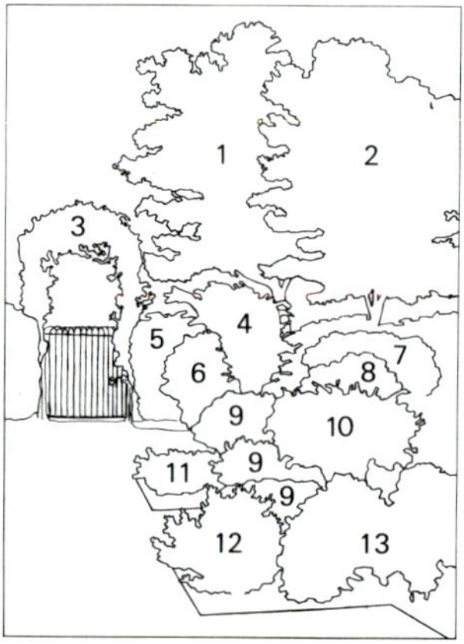

Shrubs may also be used, with hardy herbaceous perennials, in a mixed border, to add height and to give an air of permanence. Many of them will provide with their flowers or foliage a certain interest during the winter months when the herbaceous perennials will, for the most part, have been cut down.

Some shrubs, and not only the less interesting kinds, may be used for hedging purposes, those which grow about 5 feet tall as boundary hedges, for example, with lower kinds as internal hedges. For this purpose it is not always necessary to use the same kind of shrub throughout the hedge, different kinds can often be used just as effectively. Taller kinds may be used to provide screens, to block out views of neighbouring houses or other features.

Some low-growing shrubs, many of them clump forming or spreading by layers or offsets, may be used as ground-cover, to prevent the growth of weeds. Heathers and lings are good examples of these for, if closely planted, they will soon make dense ground-cover.

Shrubs, climbing by means of tendrils or with twining stems, are used to clothe walls or pergolas, and even to scramble over and hide ugly sheds and outbuildings. Others which are not true climbers may also be trained against walls.

Where a shrub border of reasonable size is being planned it is possible to plant specimens that will provide flowers throughout the entire year, without concentrating too much on spring and summer when the shrubs will be competing in colour with other garden plants. In general, where winter-flowering shrubs are being planted it is worth placing them so that they can be seen from the house and certainly be inspected closely from a pathway, for many of them have fragrant flowers.

Finally, resist the temptation to plant too closely. The small specimen received from the nursery may, in five years, be 10 feet high and as much wide. There is bound to be lots of bare ground in a shrub plantation in the early years, if shrubs are properly spaced, taking into account their ultimate spread, but this can be planted up with bulbs or temporary ground-cover plants.

Shrubs can be used in any part of the garden

Careful digging is essential before any shrubs are planted.

PREPARATION OF THE SOIL

There is little point in buying a shrub, whatever the cost of it might be, and then merely digging a hole that is large enough to take the roots, replacing the soil around it and firming it. The shrub will probably do reasonably well, but will do far better if the ground is better prepared for it. It ought to live for many years, considerably longer perhaps than the planter, if it is properly dealt with from the very beginning.

As the branch system extends, so will the root system, so that, in order to allow free development, it is necessary to dig the soil widely and reasonably deeply. Double-digging, the cultivation of the soil to two spade-depths, is not often done these days, but it does pay to cultivate deeply on heavy soils and those which, after prolonged single-spit digging, have developed a hard pan below the surface, preventing free drainage and hindering the penetration of the roots. Clay soils are notoriously difficult in this respect for, although cultivation over a period of years may have made the top foot or so easier to work, below this there may be solid clay. Digging more deeply may be arduous, but is worth it in the long run.

Soils on the chalk formations vary widely. Some may have a deep chalky loam overlying the chalk, in others there may be a mere few inches of soil under which there is solid chalk. The former soils are easy to deal with, it is the thin types that present real problems. It is often necessary to compromise by breaking up the chalk below to a depth of a foot or so and as widely as possible, using, if necessary, a pick as well as a spade.

Sandy soils and those containing much peat present few problems as far as actual digging is concerned, but the former, in particular, tend to be so well drained that they retain little moisture in dry periods and plant foods tend to be washed down into them, out of the reach of roots. This is less likely to happen on the heavier soils. All soils benefit from having extra plant foods such as garden compost dug in while they are being prepared before shrubs are planted, but none so much as light, sandy soils. The object with these is to help them to retain moisture and to provide much-needed plant foods. Both can be obtained by digging in liberal quantities of humus-forming material. Moist peat helps to retain moisture, but contains little plant food and better materials are well-rotted garden compost, leafmould,

Plants should be chosen to suit particular situations.

made from fallen leaves rotted down in a heap. Other plant matter that can be used is spent hops, old mushroom compost available in certain areas, shoddy, again available in places, or seaweed that is obtainable in coastal areas. Even rotted bracken fronds can be used since bracken is a common weed of sandy places. Failing all else, or where there is not sufficient other material, it is possible to rot down bales of straw, to be bought reasonably cheaply from farmers who have surplus stocks. The bales are broken up, sulphate of ammonia is scattered among them and the straw is thoroughly watered. It should rot down quite quickly to a dark brown material that can then be dug into the soil.

Farmyard manure is, of course, the best material of all, but so little of it is available, especially in suburban areas, that its use in liberal quantities on light soils can hardly be considered. Where it is available it may be used, mixed with compost, or by itself as a mulch or dug in, but it should be well-rotted. If it is fresh, it should be well down in the soil and not placed immediately round roots that may be scorched by it. It is better to use fresh farmyard manure to help to rot down other plant materials, or to stack it for a period until it has rotted down better. It helps to rot down straw very quickly if the manure and straw are thoroughly mixed together.

If the shrubs are not planted immediately, the sacking should be kept moist. When finally planted they should be spaced the correct distance apart.

Larger shrubs need two people to plant them, one person to hold the shrub upright while the other returns the soil around it.

PLANTING

The planting season for leaf-shedding shrubs extends from October to March, depending on the weather, and even into April if March is exceptionally bad. Evergreens are best planted either in September, so that their roots can have a chance to become active before winter sets in, or in April or early May, when root growth should start immediately, preventing the loss of leaves. If May is a hot, dry month, newly-planted evergreens may need overhead spraying each day during May and June to prevent leaf-loss, an operation that is best carried out in the cool of the evening.

The improvement of the soil before planting has already been dealt with. The actual planting may be done at any time except when the ground is frozen, snow-covered or so rain-sodden that it is difficult to work. It is worth making preparations beforehand by keeping on one side, under cover, a supply of soil that is easily workable and can be put around the roots when planting. It can be kept, until required, in a shed or outhouse or covered with plastic sheeting. It is useful to add bonemeal at the rate of about $\frac{1}{4}$ lb to a barrow-load of the mixture. Even on lighter soils, or when planting is done in drier weather, bonemeal should be forked into the soil as it is an excellent, slow-acting plant food.

Small shrubs can be planted by one person but large plants may need two people, one to hold the shrub upright while the other returns the soil round the roots and firms it. Depth of planting is important and in general the soil mark on the stem acts as a guide to planting depth. Lavenders, ericas, callunas, *Hypericum calycinum, Fuchsia magellanica, Kerria japonica, Spiraea bumalda* and other plants that make spreading clumps, may be planted a little deeper to encourage clump formation. Large specimens, with a big root formation, should be shaken while planting to ensure that soil is properly worked in among the roots to leave no air gaps. Broken or damaged roots should be cut back before planting. The planting hole should be made sufficiently large to enable undamaged roots to be spread

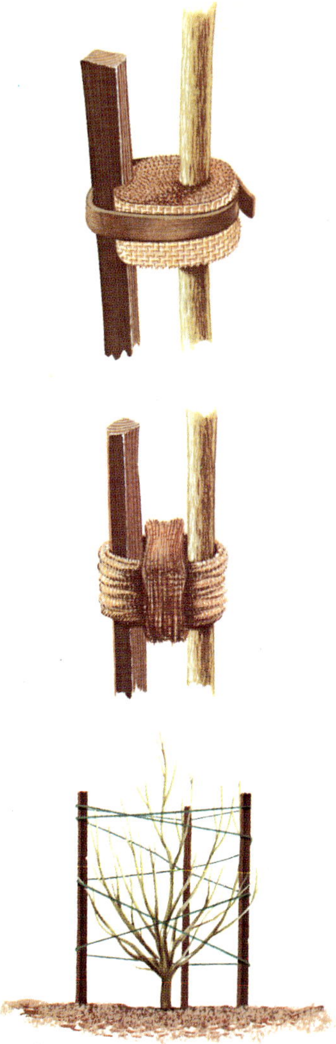

Shrubs must be staked firmly and prevented from rubbing their support, using sacking (*above*), cloth (*centre*) or twine (*below*).

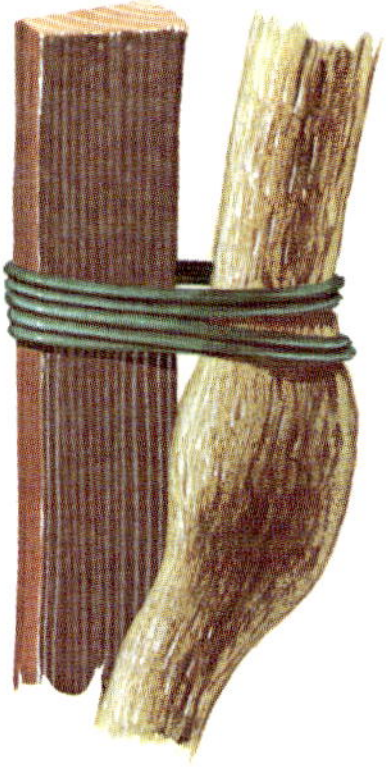

The twine should not be too tight or deformities will result (*above*). The stake should fall below the crotch of the tree.

out properly without being bent back on each other. Spreading the roots out in this way will also help to provide firm anchorage for the plant, although trees and shrubs grown on a stem should be provided with a stout stake firmly driven into the centre of the hole before planting is started. To plant firmly is essential, though this does not mean trampling round the shrub so hard that roots are broken off. Some plants, notably rhododendrons, arrive from the nursery with their fibrous roots balled in sacking. In such instances the roots should not be spread out and all that is necessary is to loosen the sacking, plant the roots in a hole large enough to take the ball, and firm the soil round them.

If the root ball looks as though it will disintegrate when the sacking is removed from around it, the plant can be put into the ground, sacking and all, merely removing the string after planting. The sacking may be pulled away after planting, but if it does not pull away easily it can be left and will soon rot down. The roots will also grow up through the sacking as it rots.

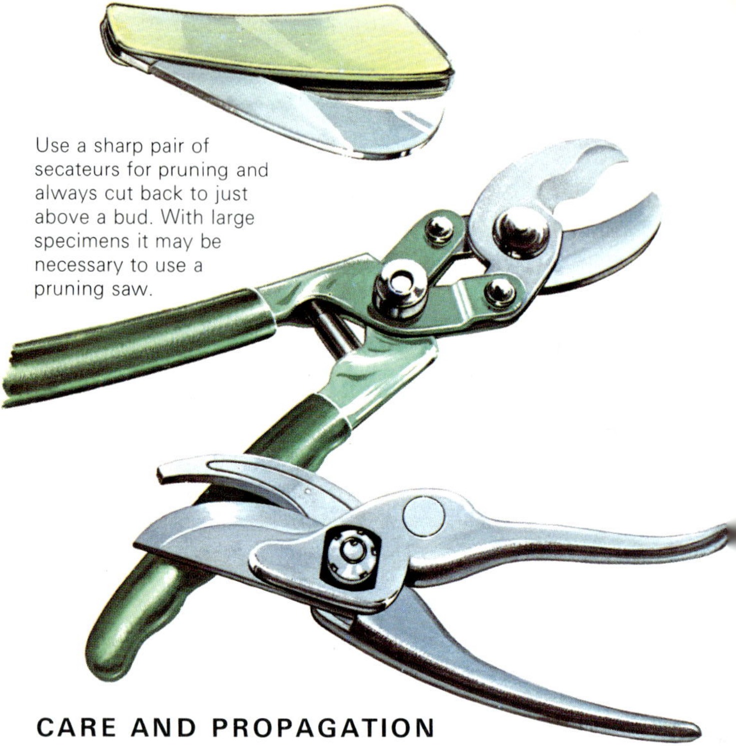

Use a sharp pair of secateurs for pruning and always cut back to just above a bud. With large specimens it may be necessary to use a pruning saw.

CARE AND PROPAGATION

Immediately after planting, damaged branches or shoots should be cut away making the cut immediately above a bud. Contrary to the beliefs held by many jobbing gardeners, many shrubs need little or no pruning at all. Certainly they do not need an annual hacking back in the winter or spring, an operation often carried out for the sake of 'tidiness' rather than to help the plant to produce more and better flowers or fruits, which should be the object of pruning. Where shrubs make reasonably symmetrical specimens in the normal course of events, there is no reason why the occasional 'wild' shoot should not be cut back, but this, like the removal of dead or dying shoots, is a mere tidying operation rather than real pruning.

Basically, shrubs may be divided into three groups: those that need no pruning; those that produce flowers in the spring on shoots made during the previous year; and those that flower in summer or autumn on shoots made in the current season. Those that flower on the previous season's growths should be pruned after the flowers have faded, cutting back those shoots that have borne flowers. Those that flower on the current season's wood are usually pruned the following spring, cutting back the old growths that flowered the previous year to within a few inches of the point where they spring from the main stem.

Many shrubs and trees, especially rhododendrons, azaleas, magnolias and camellias, benefit from an annual mulch in spring of such materials as moist peat, rotted compost or leafmould. The mulch should be spread over the soil round the shrub to a depth of several inches. It will gradually be absorbed into the soil by the action of worms or washed into the soil by rain. Any left on the surface in the autumn may be lightly forked into the top few inches of soil, taking care to avoid damage to roots near the surface.

There are several ways of propagating shrubs, although not all of them can be relied upon to give good results. It is, for instance, possible to grow many shrubs from seed, though it can be a slow process. The seeds of tree paeonies, for example, may take a year or even two years to germinate. Germination of hard-coated seeds can be hastened by stratifying them. This consists of exposing them to the action of frost and weather to help to break down the hard outer coating. The method often adopted is to place, in the autumn, a layer of sand in a flower pot or seed pan, put in a layer of seeds, add another layer of sand, another layer of seeds, until the pot or other container is full and then leave this outdoors all winter in an exposed place. By the following spring the seed coats should have rotted or partially decomposed and it is then possible to sift out the seeds from the sand and sow them. This can be done in pots of seed compost in a cold frame or cold greenhouse, or outdoors, when germination should be quite rapid.

Propagation of many shrubs by cuttings is not

The seeds of many shrubs are berries and can be collected, dried, and planted.

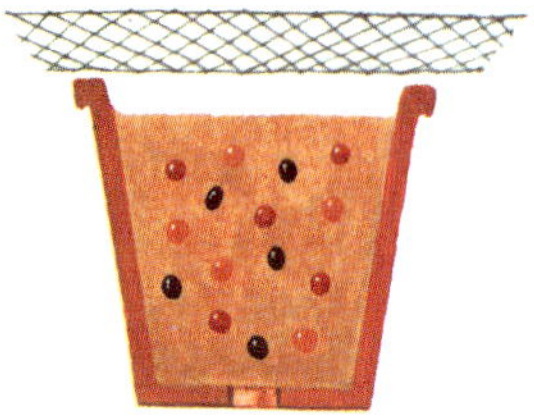

Seeds stored in sand in a flower pot can be exposed to the weather to break down the hard outer coating.

Seed boxes should be carefully labelled.

Shoots should be selected with a heel, or cut below a bud.

If the cutting is placed in a pot surrounded with polythene and watered from below it should root satisfactorily.

difficult. Cuttings of half-ripe growths may be taken in summer, and rooted in a closed propagating case in the greenhouse, in a mixture of moist sand and peat or even in pure sand. If pure sand is used the cuttings must be potted into a soil mixture as soon as roots have formed. They are then grown in pots, until they can be planted out into a nursery bed the following spring and into their permanent place the following year.

Propagation by hard-wood or naked cuttings is successful with many shrubs. These are taken in October or November and are usually 6–12 inches long. As with most cuttings, the shoots are trimmed just below a joint or bud, the lower leaves, if any remain, are removed, and the cuttings are inserted 3–4 inches deep, either in pots of sandy compost placed in a well-ventilated cold frame, or out of doors, in a sheltered position. Out of doors it is usual to make a slit in the ground with a spade, scatter sharp sand in the bottom, insert the cuttings and then firm the soil around them. By the following spring they can be lifted carefully and planted out, spaced 6–12 inches apart in a nursery bed. If evergreens are to be propagated in this way it is better to root them in a cold frame. Hormone rooting powders are available, but few gardeners require more than a small number of extra specimens and it is quite usual to expect a 50% 'strike' and not at all unusual to find that 90% of cuttings of certain shrubs have rooted.

Some shrubs are easily increased by layering their shoots. Some will even layer themselves as long shoots touch the ground and root from the point of contact. Shoots, preferably those that can easily be bent down to ground level, can be buried in the soil and, from the buds or nodes below soil level, roots should form. The rooted layer can eventually be cut off from the parent plant and start an existence of its own. With some shrubs all that is required is a long shoot

When shrubs are increased by layering their shoots success is more often assured if the woody shoot is slit just below a joint.

If a stone is placed over the point where the stem is buried in the ground it will conserve moisture below it.

bent down, buried in the soil and a stone or wire peg used to hold it in position. Success is more often assured, however, if the woody shoot is slit just below a joint, to form a 'tongue' at the point where it is buried in the soil. Alternatively, when the shoot is bent down it can be twisted and bent upwards at this point and then buried and held in place. On heavy soils it is advisable to provide a good rooting medium, such as a mixture of sand and peat, at the rooting place. A brick or stone, placed over the point where the stem is buried, is probably considerably better than a wire peg, because the soil beneath the brick will then remain moist, even in dry weather.

Division is a method of propagation often used where herbaceous perennials are concerned but is applicable to only a few shrubs, those that make masses of fibrous roots and clump-like growth, or make offsets, or sucker growth. It must be remembered that where varieties are grafted on to common stock, as in lilacs, the sucker growths will be those of the common stock, *Syringa vulgaris,* and not the desirable variety. Among the shrubs which may be propagated by division or by offsets are amelanchiers, *Fuchsia magellanica, Hypericum calycinum, Kerria japonica,* lavandulas, mahonias, rubus, certain spiraeas and syringas, remembering the proviso mentioned above.

BUYING SHRUBS

However early one orders shrubs, the arrival of the plants from the nursery is dictated by various factors not all under the control of the gardener. Accordingly, bundles of shrubs, well packed by the nursery, may arrive when it is quite impossible to plant them, perhaps because the ground is water-logged, frozen hard or covered with snow. The shrubs should be quite safe if the ties are loosened and they are left in their bundles, for two or three weeks, in a shed. But, as soon as the weather is suitable, even though it may not be convenient to carry out the actual planting, the shrubs should be removed from their bundles and heeled-in, until they can be planted out into their final places, normally not later than March.

Heeling-in consists merely of planting the shrubs temporarily. It is often recommended that a trench is dug and the roots of the plants set in this, laying them at an angle, and soil returned and firmed. It is much better, however, to choose a sheltered place, such as behind

Shrubs generally arrive from the nursery protected by sacking and straw. In bad weather they can safely be left in their bundles for about three weeks if the ties around them are loosened.

a hedge, and make a trench, planting the shrubs in this so that they are upright rather than slanting. This is because, in a bad winter, it may not be possible to move them to their permanent places until growth has well started and, when this happens, and the shrubs are laid at an angle, the new shoots will grow upright producing distorted growth.

On heavy clay soils it is a thankless task trying to heel-in shrubs and it is well worthwhile to keep a supply of friable soil mixture handy to place round the roots. Not only is this easier to handle, but it will also ensure that root development will begin without hindrance. All that remains to do then is to lift the shrubs carefully and plant them out in their permanent places after proper soil preparation.

The selection and arrangement of shrubs is very much a matter of personal choice but it is well to be guided by some general rules. In shrub borders, or other places where a number of shrubs and small trees are grown together, they should be planted in as naturalistic a manner as possible, avoiding rigidity. Rectangular shapes of beds and paths do not take full advantage of the natural symmetry of most

Heeling-in means planting temporarily. The plants are stood upright in a trench in a sheltered place.

shrubs. The natural sequence of height is trees, tall shrubs, shrubs of medium height, low growing types and finally ground-hugging kinds. Gradation of height will facilitate closer planting and give a concentration of flowers coupled with less maintenance work in weeding.

In recent years, flowering shrubs have taken an increasingly larger place in both large and small gardens. Personal likes and dislikes as regards plants vary widely but it is wise to have a plant that will grow vigorously under the conditions of the garden soil and climate. Unless the gardener is aiming at specialization in a particular group of plants, for competition purposes, for example, it is also advisable to choose shrubs that will not only blossom for a reasonable length of time but also make a decorative feature in the garden at all times of the year.

In the following pages, a variety of shrubs are discussed.

There are many shrubs that will be attractive for most of the year.

A. Syringa
B. Acer
C. Sorbus
D. Ilex

So many kinds of shrubs are now available that a selection for any type of garden should be possible. In many cases specific mention is made of varieties suitable for different types of soil, so that one can be certain of selecting the right plant for any particular area. When the specific names of hybrid races are mentioned they carry the usual multiplication sign, for example, *Berberis × rubrostilla,* but as far as possible botanical terms have been eliminated or explained immediately. If plants are being bought, it is well worthwhile obtaining them from a specialist nurseryman who stocks a wide range of plants. Many nurseries will also encourage visitors. If care is taken in the initial stages, an arrangement can be produced that will provide colour in the garden throughout the year. The choice of colour is again a personal matter and gardeners will have their own views on their favourite colour harmonies.

E. Lavandula
F. Crataegus
G. Vitis
H. Prunus

Acer palmatum heptalobum

THE POPULAR SPECIES OF SHRUBS

Acer

Most of the acers or maples are big trees, *A. pseudoplatanus,* for instance, is the Sycamore. There are, however, many others, particularly Asiatic species and their varieties, that are no more than shrubs in this country, some of them slow-growing and eventually not too big for medium-sized gardens. Most of the leaves of these plants are maple-like, that is they have five or seven deep angular lobes. In some instances these are divided yet again into numerous other segments, sometimes so narrow that the leaves look more like the fronds of a fern than the leaves of a shrub.

The Japanese Maples, varieties of *A. palmatum,* are deservedly the most popular, because they are not too large and because their leaves turn such brilliant colours in the autumn. There are many from which to choose but, if there is room for one only, *A. palmatum heptalobum* 'Osakazuki' makes a strong claim as its autumn leaves turn the brightest of scarlets. For longer-term colour, *A. p. atropurpureum* is worth considering as its foliage is a good bronze-crimson throughout the summer and there are many others that grow slowly to 5–8 feet. The species itself is more vigorous and may reach 15–20 feet. There are a few varieties of *A. japonicum,* another Japanese Maple, of which *aureum* has yellow leaves while others provide good autumn colour.

Although these Japanese Maples will tolerate chalky soils, this is not really the correct medium. They prefer ordinary, well-drained loam, with fair quantities of moist peat dug in at planting time. Cutting winds can sear them so it is best to plant them where they get some protection from wind. Frost damaged and wind damaged shoots should be cut back in late spring but unless the size must be restricted no pruning is necessary.

Propagation of the choice garden forms is usually done by grafting on to seedlings of *A. palmatum,* preferably in a greenhouse during the spring. Seeds that are saved from good forms of these Japanese Maples will usually give quite good plants but it must not be expected that they will necessarily resemble the parent plants.

Amelanchier

There seems to be a certain amount of confusion over the correct name of the plant that is usually grown in our gardens under the name of *Amelanchier canadensis*. It may strictly be *A. laevis*. Correct name apart, it is a charming large shrub or small tree, its period of beauty extending throughout much of the spring, when the young leaves break from the buds and are pink in colour, to autumn when the foliage turns an attractive red before it falls.

The white flowers, which have five narrow petals, open in April and are so freely borne that the shrub becomes a mass of white. They are followed by fruits, that are red at first but which later ripen to a reddish-purple, providing the birds leave them on the twigs long enough.

A. ovalis, the Snowy Mespilus, and *A. oblongifolia*, the Swamp Sugar Pear, are two others, better perhaps for the smaller garden than *A. laevis*, as they seldom grow much more than a dozen feet tall, whereas *A. laevis* may, in time, grow to 20 feet. *A. ovalis* is distinguished by the woolly whiteness of its young twigs and leaves. *A. oblongifolia* tends to make sucker growths, though these are seldom a nuisance and, in fact, provide an easy way of propagating as it is only necessary to dig them up in the winter and transplant them. Otherwise, the flowers and fruits are very similar indeed and the leaves of both plants colour well during the autumn.

No pruning is necessary, nor do these useful and handsome shrubs make any particular soil demands. They will grow extremely well on chalk soils and in exposed positions in the garden.

Amelanchier laevis may in time grow to over twenty feet and is not very suitable for the small garden.

Berberis

There are probably around a hundred berberises readily obtainable from nurserymen in this country, so that the choice is apt to be somewhat bewildering. In the larger garden there may be room for twenty or thirty kinds but the smaller garden cannot normally accommodate more than a few.

Darwin's Barberry, *B. darwinii,* is still one of the best. It is an evergreen, growing to 6 feet with small, holly-like leaves and clusters of orange-red flowers in May, followed by blue fruits covered with a plum-like bloom.

B. thunbergii atropurpurea, a deciduous kind, grows to about 5 feet and is very colourful when in leaf, for the foliage is reddish-purple. The flowers are pale yellow. There is a dwarf form *nana* and both these are useful for making hedges, the latter for small interior hedges.

Two good hybrids are B. × *rubrostilla*, about 4 feet high, deciduous, with very large coral fruits, and *B.* × *stenophylla,* an evergreen, up to 10 feet tall, and sometimes more than this wide. It is very free-flowering, its golden flowers appearing in late April followed by blue fruits, and makes a fine informal hedge where there is room.

These barberries are easy to grow, with no special soil requirements. Little pruning is needed, though the growth of the deciduous kinds can be thinned periodically.

A bush of *Berberis darwinii* (*bottom left*), the flowers (*right*), and the fruit (*centre*). *Berberis thunbergii atropurpurea* (*bottom right*).

Buddleia

Buddleias, at least those commonly grown, which are varieties of *B. davidii* (*B. variabilis*), must be about the easiest of shrubs to grow. Perhaps because of this they are all too often neglected, and bushes 12–15 feet tall are seen producing flowers at the top and little or nothing lower down. This is one of those shrubs that flower on wood made the same year and if it is cut back in late winter it will send up new growths of varying lengths, each bearing their quota of heavily fragrant flower-spikes, covered with butterflies in late summer. There are numerous varieties in colours such as deep violet 'Black Night', lavender pink 'Charming', deep purple 'Dubonnet', lilac pink 'Pink Pearl', reddish-purple 'Royal Red' and white varieties such as 'White Bouquet' and 'White Cloud'.

B. globosa, known as the Orange Ball Tree, is a contrast, because its orange-yellow flowers, borne in May, are ball shaped and dangle from the branches. This grows to 12–15 feet and should be pruned after flowering, shortening the shoots that have borne flowers to about half their length.

There are many other buddleias, many of them too tender for most gardens. *B.* × *weyeriana* is a bit different and is a hybrid derived from the two previously described. This has ball-like flower-heads, mainly yellow and orange, but flushed or shaded with pink or mauve.

A bush of *Buddleia davidii,* Royal Red variety, (*left*) and flowers (*right*), with those of *Buddleia globosa,* the Orange Ball tree.

Calluna vulgaris, variety H. E. Beale

Calluna

Calluna vulgaris, the single species in the genus, is the common Heather or Ling, that makes so many of our hills and moors colourful from late summer to autumn. In the wild the plant has purplish-pink flowers, but it is so variable that nurserymen specializing in heathers may list up to fifty different kinds, varying in height from 3–4 inches to 2 feet and showing great colour variation, both in flowers and foliage. Some have double flowers and the best of these is

'H. E. Beale', flowering late, growing to about 2 feet, with tall spikes of rosy-pink flowers. If a dwarf double is required then it can be found in 'J. H. Hamilton', about 9 inches tall, with pink flowers.

The variety *searlei* has fine white flowers and there is a variety of this with golden leaves, called *searlei aurea. C. v. aurea* is another golden-leaved form, not so tall. In *C. v. argentea* the young growths are silvery. *C. v. nana* is one of the lowest growing, with purple flowers.

These callunas must have lime-free soil and they do best where the soil is dry and the position open and sunny. Plant them fairly closely together in drifts or clumps so that they grow together to make a continuous mat, to keep down weeds. A light clip over with shears after flowering will encourage new growth to form, and keep the plants neat and compact.

Calluna vulgaris aurea, a gold-leaved form

Camellia

The camellias are not difficult to grow provided they can be given the right conditions. They do not like chalky soils and although they will grow in exposed sites their buds are liable to be damaged by searing winds and spring frosts. Light woodland places are ideal or, in colder gardens, a place against a south, west or even north, but not east, wall. They make good tub plants, either for terraces or cold conservatories and this gives the gardener who has chalky soil a chance to enjoy these delightful plants.

Unless your garden is in one of the milder counties, stick to the varieties of *C. japonica* and the newer hybrids, the *williamsii* group, which are as hardy as any other shrub. The *japonica* forms vary in colour from white to rich crimson and there are kinds with single, semi-double and fully double flowers. The *williamsii* hybrids have excellent single or semi-double flowers. They appear to grow a little more quickly than the *japonica* forms, but both reach about 12–15 feet, the latter growing taller in ideal conditions. Both should begin to flower in late February or early March.

Dig in moist peat and leafmould before planting and mulch the shrubs each spring with the same materials.

Camellia × williamsii

Camellia japonica makes a delightful tub plant

The hybrid *Caryopteris* × *clandonensis* has small bright blue flowers carried in clusters.

Caryopteris

Shrubs which do not grow too tall, nor take up too much space, are decided assets for the small garden. Caryopteris, members of the Verbena family (*Verbenaceae*) come into this category and combine these assets with that of bearing blue flowers, uncommon in shrubs.

The most popular is *C.* × *clandonensis,* a hybrid that originated at Clandon, in Surrey, nearly 40 years ago. It can grow to about 5 feet tall, but it is easy to keep it to half this height or a little more, by cutting back each April the growths made the previous year, to within two buds of their base. New shoots quickly appear and in late summer will be bearing masses of small bright blue flowers which are carried in clusters springing from the axils of the leaves.

Even newer is 'Heavenly Blue', a hybrid from America, which makes a somewhat more upright bush, better, perhaps, for confined spaces, and with flowers of a slightly deeper blue.

Apart from these hybrids there is *C. mongholica,* a species introduced from China well over a century ago. It, too, has rich blue flowers, but is rather too tender for most gardens and, in any case, seems to be short-lived.

These caryopteris, sometimes called Blue Spiraeas or Bluebeard, because of the fringed flowers, do best in sheltered positions in full sun, though any reasonable garden soil, not too heavy, will suit them.

This shrub can grow to about 5 feet

Ceratostigma

Ceratostigma willmottianum, the species usually grown, is a hardy Plumbago. Its rich blue flowers, produced in clusters, much resemble those of the true Plumbago, that is often seen in conservatories and which has flowers that are a paler blue.

This shrub is perfectly hardy and can be grown in the open garden, where it makes a plant about 18 inches tall, its flowers beginning to appear soon after midsummer and continuing until September or October. The growths are usually cut by frost in the open garden, but no permanent damage results and it is only necessary to give the plant a trim over in April to remove the frost-killed shoots and new growth will soon start to appear. This in fact is the only form of pruning required.

Against a sunny, sheltered wall *C. willmottianum* may reach 3 feet in height and is less liable to frost damage. Another good place to grow it is in the herbaceous border, for its blue flowers associate well with the yellows and reds of the later summer border plants.

The foliage is a bonus for in the autumn it turns yellow and red, adding to the colourfulness of this useful shrub. It will grow in any kind of soil, including those containing much chalk. Plants may be lifted and divided for propagation purposes in much the same way as herbaceous perennials.

Ceratostigmas have rich clusters of deep blue flowers. One of the most popular species is *C. willmottianum* (*above*).

The Judas Tree (*Cercis siliquastrum*) has purple-pink pea flowers (*below*).

Cercis

Cercis siliquastrum is the Judas Tree, sometimes seen as a tree 20–25 feet tall, sometimes as a shrub, reaching about 12–15 feet. It ought to be grown more often, as it is perfectly hardy and is a very fine sight when in full flower in May, just before the leaves are fully open. At that time each twig carries its quota of purple-pink pea flowers and these often appear in little clusters on the trunks of older-established plants. Purplish seed-pods, 3–4 inches long, follow the flowers.

Even out of flower the shrub is attractive for the greenish-grey leaves are round, almost heart-shaped. There is a white-flowered form, *alba*, where the leaves are paler in colour.

The Judas Tree does not require special soil and needs only a sunny situation to settle down, although it is best established from a pot as, like some other pea-flowered shrubs, it does not like root disturbance. Seeds germinate readily in pots of John Innes Seed Compost.

The related Western Redbud, *C. occidentalis,* is seen even less often because it is a tender shrub and prefers the milder conditions of western areas. It reaches about 15 feet and has bright green, kidney-shaped leaves and rose-coloured flowers. *C. canadensis,* the Red-Bud, is a hardier variety, but its rosy-pink flowers are smaller than those of the Judas Tree and the latter is to be preferred if there is room for only one to be grown.

Chaenomeles

Gardeners will always refer to this shrub as the 'Japonica', so deep-rooted is this old name. It is usually seen trained as a wall shrub, 8–10 feet tall, occasionally more, and it will cover a fairly wide area if it is properly looked after. If it is grown in this way, some pruning is absolutely essential to control the vigour of the plant development and to keep it from straggling. Basically the pruning consists of cutting away any forward-pointing branches as well as any very thin growths that are produced. Cutting back of new side-growths to 5 or 6 inches is also necessary, unless they are needed as extensions or to fill in a blank space on the wall. This is done during the summer and should be combined with tying in

Chaenomeles speciosa produces attractive flowers from January until June.

the new growths to nails set in the wall or on to any other support such as trellis-work or the side of an out-building or garden shed.

The $1\frac{1}{2}$ inch wide flowers, produced on the leafless stems from January onwards, until May or June, are very attractive. Good colour forms are 'Apple Blossom', *nivalis,* white, *atrococcinea,* deep crimson, *cardinalis,* salmon-pink, and *rosea flore-plena,* which is a rose-pink, double variety. All these plants are varieties of *C. speciosa,* which is also known as *C. lagenaria* and *Cydonia japonica*. Apart from their use on walls the different varieties may be grown as open-ground shrubs, when less pruning is needed. They may also be used for hedging purposes but if this is the case they will need cutting back to keep them tidy and to prevent them from becoming too open. Whatever variety is chosen, none requires any special soil medium and will grow well on chalk. Oddly-shaped fruits, like those of the related quinces are very often produced and may be used for making such things as quince jelly.

Choisya

There is one species only of this plant, *C. ternata,* more familiar to gardeners as the Mexican Orange Blossom, because of the scented white flowers it produces in clusters in May and June, though the fragrance is definitely not that of orange-blossom.

It is an evergreen, with somewhat leathery leaves, made up of three leaflets. A well-grown plant will reach about 6 feet in height but rarely more even in the warmer parts of the country and scarcely less even in the colder districts. If it is allowed ample room it may be as wide as it is high, except in shady places when it is inclined to become straggly. For this reason it is better grown in the open, although some shelter is desirable from the cutting winds, which may damage the foliage in winter. In spring it may also be affected by late frosts.

This is a good plant for chalk, but will grow on any kind of soil, even the sandy, peaty soils on which rhododendrons thrive. Usually it makes a rounded bush, well-clothed to the ground, and no pruning is needed. Occasional 'wild' shoots may appear to spoil the symmetry and these may be cut away.

Choisya ternata is better known as the Mexican Orange Blossom.

The hybrid *Cistus × purpureus*, bush (*above*) and flowers (*below*). (*Opposite*) The Silver Pink variety is one of the hardiest hybrids.

Cistus

The cistus are the Rock Roses, plants from the Mediterranean region and, like so many others from that area, they prefer sunny places and dry, well-drained soils. They are beautiful shrubs, but even the hardiest of them are only on the borderline of hardiness, except in sheltered and warm gardens. In less well-favoured places some will survive for several years, but it is a wise precaution to take late summer cuttings and root them in bottom heat, overwintering them until they can be planted out in late spring.

One of the hardiest is the hybrid 'Silver Pink', a name which aptly describes the colour of its 3 inch wide flowers. This grows to 2 feet, or a little more. *C.* × *purpureus* is another hybrid, with beautiful purplish-crimson flowers, with a dark blotch at the base of each petal. This grows up to 6 feet high with a proportionate spread. The hardiest species is *C. laurifolius,* which again may reach to 6 feet, and has clusters of white flowers with yellow blotches at the bases of the petals.

In mild places it is worth trying other species and hybrids of these charming shrubs. Their individual flowers are usually over by noon on the day they open, but so many are borne in succession during June and July that the plants are never out of flower.

Clematis

This is another of those large genera that is bewildering in the variety it has to offer, for there are over 150 species and hybrids available of these pretty and indispensable climbers. Usually they are planted against walls, but there are so many other places where they can be accommodated that even in a small garden room might be found for several kinds. They are, for instance, excellent plants for pergolas or archways. The less vigorous kinds may be planted so that they scramble over low-growing and otherwise not particularly valuable shrubs, while the more vigorous kinds will climb up into taller trees.

Clematis montana (*left*) flowers in the spring and (*above*) the rich purple *C.* × *jackmanii* is a popular hybrid.

Cultivation is not difficult. Contrary to old gardeners' tales, lime or chalk in the soil is not essential and clematis do well on soils not containing chalk or lime, provided they are rich in plant foods. Clematis especially need more moisture-retentive soils, even heavy clay, provided it is well dug and broken up and plant foods are incorporated. What clematis do like is to have their roots cool and shaded, which means that they can be planted against shady walls, but, if so, they will send up their flowering shoots into the sunlight. So, it is better to plant them in sunny places and ensure the roots are cool. This can be arranged, if pieces of stone are placed over them, or if low-growing shrubs are planted in front of them. The soil should be enriched when digging and an annual mulch of rotted manure, leafmould, or compost given. They must be watered in dry weather, especially in spring and early summer.

Of the many kinds available, the old rich purple *C.* × *jackmanii* is still deservedly popular. 'Ville de Lyon' is a dark carmine-red flowering in late summer, and *C. montana rubens* is a pink form of the popular white *C. montana* flowering in spring. 'Comtesse de Bouchaud', pink, is one of the most free-flowering while 'Duchess of Edinburgh' is a double white but not a very vigorous kind. 'Lasursten' is one of the most popular of the large-flowered hybrids, with purple-blue flowers in summer.

Ville de Lyon is a late summer-flowering variety.

Clerodendrum trichotomum.
Leaves and flowers (*below*) and outline of bush (*opposite*).

Clerodendrum

There is always a certain attraction about shrubs with blue berries and *Clerodendrum trichotomum* is one of the finest in this category, with turquoise-blue fruits, their colour enhanced by the crimson calyces in which they are held. The fruits turn black in time and drop off, but the calyces persist to give a certain amount of colour to this hardy shrub.

It grows to some 12 feet tall, perhaps even reaching 15 feet and so requires a fair amount of space. The leaves are large, about 9 inches long, oval in shape and have a somewhat unpleasant smell if they are handled. On the other hand the white flowers are sweetly scented. These appear from July onwards, in clusters, and are tubular in shape. The red calyces surrounding them add a good deal of colour.

This shrub will grow in most garden soils, but it does not like drought, so it pays to dig in a fair amount of leaf-mould, well-rotted garden compost, or moist peat, when the ground is prepared for planting. Although it is hardy, it does best in a sheltered situation where its young shoots are not liable to be damaged by cold winds.

Pruning, in the normal sense, is not required, but it is worth going over the shrub in late spring and cutting away dead wood or shoots affected by frost. Suckers appear round the base and may be dug up and used to form new plants.

Cornus

For some reason the dogwoods are not very common in gardens in this country, yet they are attractive shrubs, not difficult to grow. Some are grown for their flowers, others for their coloured bark, and some for a combination of their flowers and richly coloured autumn leaves. Seen most often is *Cornus mas,* the Cornelian Cherry, with its small yellow flowers in February and March that are sometimes followed by bright red berries.

There are more spectacular dogwoods, such as *C. kousa chinensis,* a shrub in which the individual flowers are tiny, but surrounded by large white bracts. In autumn the leaves turn a good crimson. Some peat or leafmould dug into the soil helps this shrub, which otherwise, like most of its relations, does not require special soil.

Among those grown for the beauty of their bark, especially in winter when they are leafless, are *C. alba sibirica,* with bright red shoots, *C. stolonifera,* dark dull red shoots, and its variety *flaviramea,* with yellow bark. *C. alba* also has some varieties with attractively variegated leaves. The kinds grown for their bark need cutting back hard each spring, practically to ground level and plenty of new shoots 4–5 feet long will appear afterwards to provide winter colour.

The flowers of *Cornus kousa chinensis (above)* are tiny, surrounded by large white bracts. *Cornus alba sibirica* (*below*) is often grown for the beauty of its bark.

Cotoneaster

Although the white flowers of cotoneasters are not individually spectacular they are usually borne freely in clusters. However, these plants are not grown for flowers as much as for the brilliance of their autumn fruits and the rich colours of their autumn leaves. There are many of these plants, most of them shrubs, ranging in height from a few inches to 20 feet, with one or two which may be classed as small trees, reaching 25 feet in time.

Some take up little space and are, therefore, perfectly suitable for small gardens. The most popular of these is the Fishbone Cotoneaster, *C. horizontalis,* its branches borne in herringbone formation. It is often planted by a wall, against which it will grow up to several feet, even on a north aspect, spreading itself almost flat against the bricks. In the open, over a rock or tree stump, or planted by the side of an inspection cover, it will spread fairly horizontally. The flowers are not particularly beautiful, although they cover the shoots and are attractive to insects, but the berries are bright red and the small leaves turn red and orange before falling.

C. dielsianus grows to about 6 feet and has arching branches, bright scarlet berries and brightly coloured autumn leaves. *C. dammeri* is even better for planting beside an inspection cover for its long growths are quite prostrate, its leaves are evergreen and the freely-borne fruits are bright red. For sheer spectacle there is little to surpass in autumn 'Cornubia', an evergreen hybrid, growing to 15–20 feet, its branches laden down with its scarlet fruits. This shrub is among the largest of the cultivated cotoneasters. *C. salicifolius,* is a 12–15 feet tall, evergreen species that also fruits heavily. The variety *floccosus* has narrower leaves and big crops of small fruits while the *fructuluteo* variety is distinct in having yellow fruits. *C. simonsii,* semi-evergreen, is a species that is often used for hedging or screening purposes. It grows to about 15 feet tall eventually and is of rather stiff, upright habit usually bearing plenty of scarlet fruits.

Cotoneaster horizontalis is suitable for small gardens. The hybrid Cornubia has branches laden with scarlet fruit in autumn.

These cotoneasters are easy to grow in any kind of soil, in sun or a semi-shade. They are perfectly hardy, even in windswept coastal conditions. None need pruning, other than removing dead wood. They may seed themselves in favourable situations, but are hardly likely to become a nuisance.

The blossoms of the Double Crimson Thorn, *Crataegus oxyacantha coccinea plena*.

Crataegus

This genus contains the well-known hawthorns, quicks or Mays, useful for informal hedges and a magnificent sight when they foam with white flowers in May, but not really ornamental shrubs in the normal way. However, there is a very fine form of one of the hawthorns, *C. oxyacantha,* known botanically as *coccinea plena*, but possibly better recognized by gardeners as the Double Crimson Thorn. This makes a neat, round-headed tree, about 15 feet in height, useful as a lawn specimen or for a position perhaps by the garden gate. Two, one on each side of the gate, with their heads allowed to grow together, would be even better, especially when they produce their long-lasting crimson flowers in May and June. No pruning is needed except to remove dead wood or straying growths that would otherwise spoil the symmetrical shape. The plant is native to the British Isles and will grow in almost any situation.

There are plenty of other crataegus, some, such as *C. monogyna aurea,* a variant of the common May, with yellow fruits. Others, such as *C. arnoldiana,* have very large fruits, as big as cherries, while those of *C. arkansana*, are even bigger. *C. arnoldiana*, incidentally, is fearsomely armed, its thorns sometimes 3 inches long.

One of the daintiest of this genus is *C. tanacetifolia,* the Tansy-leaved Thorn, with attractive deeply-lobed grey-green leaves and large flowers, up to an inch across. The yellow fruits have the same diameter, hanging like small apples. This eventually makes a taller tree than most of these crataegus, reaching about 30 feet in height.

The round trees are suitable for lawns.

Cytisus battandieri (below) needs wall protection in most gardens.

Cytisus

Not all gardens are blessed with good soil and, while it is possible to improve the soil, this is often a lengthy process. Meanwhile, it is worth planting those shrubs that not only put up with poor conditions, but actually thrive on them. Among these are the cytisus, which, like the genistas and *Spartium junceum* described elsewhere, are called brooms. They are very much shrubs for dry, stony, well-drained soils.

There are many cytisus, in a wide range of colours, and among the finest are those in which the pea-shaped flowers are of two colours, the standard, back petal, of one colour, the wing petals another. In some the petals are streaked with other colours. Habits vary greatly and some kinds such as *C. decumbens,* with bright yellow flowers, are prostrate in growth, while others, such as the white-flowered *C. albus* and 'Johnson's Crimson', with clear crimson blooms, may reach 6 or 7 feet. The Moroccan Broom, *C. battandieri,* grows even taller, reaching 15–20 feet, but it needs wall protection in most gardens. However, it is one of the finest, with silvery leaves and upright spikes of yellow flowers in July.

Most brooms tend to become straggly unless they are pruned after they have flowered. Light pruning of the stems that have carried blooms is all that is needed.

Cytisus scoparius

Daphne

The daphne most usually seen is our native *D. mezereum*, the Mezereon, now rare as a native plant, but easily obtainable from nurseries. It is an old 'cottage garden' plant, grown for the sake of its sweetly-scented purplish-red flowers, that smother the twigs in February and March and often into April. Round red fruits follow in autumn and these provide a ready means of increase. It grows about 4 feet tall, tolerating most soils, except very dry ones, and it does well on the chalk and in partially shaded situations. There is a fine white-flowered variety *alba,* a pink form *rosea,* and a form, *grandiflora*, producing larger flowers a good deal earlier.

Not all daphnes are so easy to grow. *Daphne × burkwoodii,* a semi-evergreen hybrid, about 3 feet tall, with very fragrant pale pink flowers in May and June, is not at all difficult. It is also worth trying the variegated leaf form, *D. odora aureo-marginata*. This is harder than the species and is an evergreen, slow-growing to perhaps 3 feet, although much depends on soil and situation. Like other exotic daphnes, it prefers a well-drained, though moisture-retaining loam. Peat and leafmould dug in before planting may do something towards ensuring success with this aristocratic plant, although shelter from frosts and cutting winds is probably more important.

None of the daphnes described here requires pruning, unless it is to remove frost-killed wood.

Daphne × burkwoodii, a semi-evergreen hybrid.

Sweetly-scented *Daphne mezereum* (*above*) with outline of the shrub.

Deutzia

The deutzias flower in June, at about the same time as the philadelphus and, although their flowers lack the sweet fragrance of those of the best of the mock oranges, they are worth planting for their beauty. They are easy to grow and are not too big for small gardens as the tallest reaches only about 10 feet and most of them have a maximum height of 6 feet. Some varieties can be bought that are not much more than 4 feet tall.

One of the best is *D. scabra candidissima*, about 10 feet tall, with pure white double flowers. 'Pride of Rochester' (*D. scabra plena*) is another good double-flowered kind, the petals rosy-purple on the outside and white within. 'Perle

Deutzia Perle Rose is suitable for restricted spaces.

Rose' is only 6 feet tall and, therefore, suitable for more restricted spaces and has flowers that are a soft rose-pink. *D. gracilis,* 3–4 feet, with graceful arching stems, has white flowers and is the kind forced into flower for sale in florists' shops. *D.* × *elegantissima,* which grows to 5–6 feet, is exceptional in having fragrant flowers, clear rosy-pink in colour.

Some pruning is needed with these shrubs. They produce most of their flowers on shoots made during the previous year, so that immediately after flowering a proportion of the older branches should be cut away. It is inadvisable to cut away too many for from them may spring new shoots to flower the following season.

Deutzia scabra plena is a double flowered kind that is easily cultivated.

Erica carnea (left) and
Erica vagans (right)

Erica

The callunas described earlier are usually referred to as lings or heathers but their close relations, the ericas, which have given their name to the whole family (*Ericaceae*) are also known as heathers, or heaths. Whereas there is but one species of calluna there are over 500 erica species, although most of these are of little importance to the shrub gardener as they are tender, greenhouse plants from South Africa.

There is a wide range of hardy ericas, however, mostly from Europe, including the British Isles and, by choosing the right kinds, it is possible to have them in flower throughout the twelve months of the year. Like the lings, they make fine ground cover if planted fairly closely together so that they eventually merge. Heights range from a few inches to a maximum of about 2 feet with the exception of the 'tree heaths'. There is a good colour variation and some differences in foliage colour.

Callunas may be grown only on lime-free soil, but there are one or two ericas that will grow perfectly well on chalky, or limey soils, which is a great help to the thousands of gardeners who have to put up with these soils. The same kinds will also grow on any other soil, so it is worth describing them first. The principal species is *E. carnea,* about a foot tall, with rosy-purple flowers from December to April. There are numerous varieties of this, some, such as 'Eileen Porter', flowering from October onwards and bearing carmine flowers, others, such as *vivellii,* are dwarfer. Colours include rosy-red, shades of pink, dark red, carmine and white.

The hybrid *E.* × *darleyensis* is also lime-tolerant. It grows to 18 inches tall and has rose-coloured flowers from November onwards until March or April. It has one or two varieties, including the white-flowered 'Silberschmelz'. One parent is *E. carnea,* the other *E. mediterranea* which is a good deal taller, at least 4 feet and in favoured places nearer 8 feet. It has rosy-red flowers from March or April, into June, so extending the season for these lime-tolerant heaths.

There is a wide range of others for lime-free soils, including several 'tree heaths' and the Cornish Heath *E. vagans* which will reach 2 feet. As far as the lower-growing kinds are concerned pruning is best carried out after flowering. It consists in trimming the plants lightly after the flowers have faded. Less vigorous kinds need no pruning. All need a sunny site on well-drained soil and should be planted firmly.

Erica mediterranea will grow to four feet and has red flowers from March until June.

Escallonia

The finest escallonias are seen by the sea, where *E. macrantha* is often used as a hedging plant. Its rosy-crimson flowers, which have a honey fragrance, set among the dark green leaves are a familiar sight in the late spring and summer of most coastal areas. It is most particularly found in the south and west of England.

The escallonias are, with few exceptions, evergreen shrubs, although they tend to be semi-evergreen in colder areas, where they are best given the shelter of a wall. They all do well near the sea, although some of them are hardy enough to be grown in inland gardens. Among the hardiest are *E.* × *langleyensis,* a hybrid with rosy carmine flowers, that grows to about 5–6 feet, or up to 10 feet near the coast. *E.* × *edinensis*, another not quite so tall hybrid, has rosy-pink flowers, while 'Slieve Donard', apple-blossom pink in colour, is one of a number of hybrids developed at a well-known nursery in Northern Ireland, in various shades of pink.

In general, escallonias do not require special soil, though they do best in rich loam. They make good hedges and in coastal areas grow densely enough to form excellent windbreaks. Their growths tend to be somewhat arching and, if neglected, straggly, but this can be controlled by hard pruning, which entails cutting off flowered shoots once the flowers are over. Half-ripe cuttings, taken in August, will oot readily in bottom heat.

Escallonia × langleyensis is one of the hardiest escallonias and will grow to ten feet under good conditions.

Eucryphia

There are not many of these beautiful shrubs and two only have any claim to hardiness. One of these is the species *E. glutinosa,* which makes a deciduous shrub about 12–15 feet tall, or is occasionally seen as a small tree. It will not do well on lime or chalky soils, but will flourish in the southern counties, at least, on any reasonably rich loamy soil, if given a sheltered position. It bears from July onwards, beautiful fragrant white flowers, 2 inches or more across, with a central boss of stamens. In the autumn the leaves turn to rich colours before falling.

The other hardy kind is the evergreen hybrid, *E.* × *nymansay,* a cross between *E. glutinosa* and a less hardy species, *E. cordifolia. E.* × *nymansay* is a vigorous shrub which may reach 25 feet or more, but takes up less room than one might think as it is seldom more than 10 feet wide and would therefore not be out of place in a medium-sized garden. It produces its handsome flowers, which are like large white single roses with a central mass of yellow stamens, during August and September. Unlike its parents, *E.* × *nymansay* will tolerate lime or chalk in the soil, but it is not a shrub for thin soils overlying chalk. It will tolerate a deep chalky loam, but it does appreciate some shelter, particularly in its young state.

Eucryphias need no pruning unless it is to remove dead or frost-damaged wood, an operation best carried out in April or May.

Flowers of the hybrid *Eucryphia* × *nymansay (above)* and the shrub form (*left*).

Forsythia

The spring garden would be incomplete without the golden-yellow flowers of the forsythias. These are among the hardiest and easiest of shrubs to grow, and for that reason are sometimes neglected, when a little attention would produce even better results. In general hard pruning is not necessary. Particularly in open situations in colder gardens, however, the tips of the shoots made the previous year, on which most of the flowers are borne, sometimes die back and to prevent these from looking bare it is a good plan to cut them back. Apart from this these shrubs need little pruning other than the occasional cutting out of the oldest wood.

Those grown in the open are usually forms or varieties of the hybrid, *F.* × *intermedia,* of which the best variety is perhaps the modern 'Lynwood', with large, golden-yellow flowers that are freely borne. 'Beatrix Farrand' has flowers nearly as large and makes an upright bush. *F. spectabilis*, the kind usually seen, also blooms freely, although its flowers are not so large. An interesting kind is 'Arnold Dwarf' which makes a low spreading bush, 6 feet or so across, but only 2 feet or so high.

Forsythia suspensa is another fine species, but although it can be grown in the open, the best position is against a south or west wall, trained as a wall shrub, where it will grow 10 feet tall or more, producing lemon-yellow flowers along its arching branches.

These shrubs will grow in any ordinary garden soil.

Forsythia suspensa (opposite) and the hybrid *Forsythia* × *intermedia* (*above*) which has large, freely borne, golden-yellow flowers.

Fuchsia magellanica (below) and its varieties are hardy enough to survive outdoors in most places and it is not uncommon to see it grown as a hedge.

Fuchsia

Most of the fuchsias are not hardy enough to qualify for inclusion in a book devoted to describing shrubs that are hardy in these islands. However, *F. magellanica* and its varieties and one or two others, are certainly hardy enough to survive outdoors in most places, even though in less favoured gardens they may be cut to the ground by frost each year. *F. magellanica* will grow where frosts are less severe and has red and purple flowers that are very freely borne. It may reach 10 feet and it is not uncommon to see it grown as a delightful flowering hedge in the West. Cut by frost it seldom fails to recover, sending up new stems from the base, but will then only grow to about 5 feet in height.

The variety usually grown is *riccartonii,* with crimson and purple flowers. There is a white flowered variety *alba,* one rather more slender in growth, *gracilis,* sometimes classed as a species, and also one (*versicolor*) in which the leaves are variegated with crimson, pink and cream. This does not grow so tall. 'Mrs. Popple' is another hardy fuchsia, with larger flowers, scarlet and deep purple in colour, while 'Madame Cornelissen' has attractive crimson and white flowers.

These hardy fuchsias will grow in any ordinary soil and sunny position. Except in very exposed gardens, where a covering of bracken will help, there is no need to give them extra protection; if they are damaged by frost it is a simple matter to cut the stems down to ground level in spring.

Garrya

The only species that is commonly grown is *Garrya elliptica*, which is sometimes, for reasons that are obvious when the plant is in flower, known as the Silk Tassel Bush. It comes from North America and is quite hardy in most parts of the country, although in the North and East it does better if given the protection of a wall. It grows rapidly and in a few years will reach 12–15 feet in height and a well-grown plant may be 6–8 feet wide.

It is not the flowers themselves that make the plant so attractive, but the long, silvery-green catkins in which they

Garrya elliptica will cover a wall even in a shady position.

The flowers give it the name of Silk Tassel Bush.

are borne. These, on male plants, may reach a foot long and they make the shrub a most handsome specimen when it is in full flower. The catkins start to appear in November and are very much in evidence until late in February.

This is an easily grown shrub flourishing well on poor soils as well as on chalk or in sea-side gardens. It does not object to a shady position, thus making it suitable for a north or east wall, and does not need pruning. Perhaps the only point which can be made against it is that it is not easy to transplant, and is best planted out, as a young specimen, from a pot. If you grow one plant only get the male, for the catkins of the female plant are much shorter.

Genista

The genistas are among those plants popularly referred to as brooms, the others are the cytisus and *Spartium junceum,* the Spanish broom. Whereas the pea-shaped flowers of cytisus may be of various colours, those of genistas, with very few exceptions, are yellow or golden-yellow. There are other slight botanical differences, although the two genera are closely related.

One of the most spectacular when it is in full flower in July is the Mount Etna broom, *G. aethnensis,* which may grow to 12 feet or more tall, with long drooping shoots, clothed with small golden-yellow flowers.

By contrast, *G. lydia* seldom exceeds 2 feet in height although its growths are equally drooping in habit and hidden beneath golden-yellow flowers in May and June.

The Spanish Gorse, *G. hispanica,* is another dwarf kind, about 2 feet tall, sometimes less and sometimes a little more. It is very spiny and equally floriferous, with golden-yellow flowers appearing at about the same time or a little later than those of *G. lydia*.

Genista lydia

The attractive flowers (*above*) and bush (*opposite*) of *Genista aethnensis*.

There are other, mostly dwarf, varieties, although one good exception is *G. cinerea*, some 8 feet tall, with greyish leaves and fragrant yellow flowers in June and July.

These genistas do well in poor dry soil but must have full sun. Prune them after flowering, cutting away those stems that have carried blooms, but avoiding cutting into the older wood. Always plant them out from pots as they resent root disturbance.

Hamamelis mollis
with the outline of its
shrub form.

Hamamelis

The Hamamelis are the Wych Hazels or Witch Hazels as they are perhaps better known and are very valuable because they flower in winter, on the leafless branches. These shrubs grow slowly, but will eventually reach a height of 10 feet or more, with a proportionate spread and so require a fair amount of room. However, in order that the flowers and their fragrance can be appreciated, it is well worth planting them fairly near a pathway.

H. mollis is probably the best of the genus and it produces flowers from late December until late February or early March. These are golden-yellow blossoms, with strap-shaped petals that are about $\frac{1}{2}$ inch in length. The leaves are large and turn bright orange in autumn before falling. There is a variety, *pallida,* with paler flowers.

H. japonica in contrast has less fragrant flowers and the narrow petals are wavy with the flowers surrounded by red bracts. It flowers at about the same time as *H. mollis* and has one or two varieties, including *arborea,* which is considerably taller, and *zuccariniana* with flowers of lemon-yellow. There is a variety 'Carmine Red', so called because of the colour of its flowers and another variety 'Hiltingbury' from the hybrid *H.* × *intermedia,* which has coppery-red flowers. 'Copper Beauty', sometimes known as 'Jelena', has flowers of coppery-orange.

These wych hazels do well in any ordinary garden soil, are perfectly hardy and need no pruning other than the normal trimming necessary to keep the shrub in shape.

Hebe

These are the Shrubby Veronicas, still sometimes listed in catalogues under Veronica, though the name Hebe has now become more familiar to gardeners. Certainly it serves to distinguish these evergreen shrubs from their hardy herbaceous relatives.

There are many varieties, most of them from New Zealand, but not all are hardy and it is unfortunate that the tender ones have the brightest coloured flowers. However, the hardier kinds are beautiful, free-flowering shrubs and well worth their place. One of the finest that is known is 'Midsummer Beauty' that reaches about 4 feet tall. 'Autumn Glory', which actually comes into flower in summer and goes on until October, makes a widespread bush, about $1\frac{1}{2}$ feet high, with rich violet-blue flowers carried in short spikes. *H. brachysiphon* (*H. traversii*) is the commonest kind, often used for hedging purposes in coastal areas, but a fine specimen by itself when given room to develop. It reaches 5–6 feet and has multitudes of white flowers in short spikes. 'White Gem' is an improved dwarf form.

H. elliptica, also useful for hedging, is reasonably hardy. This makes a symmetrical, dome-shaped shrub and has mauve or sometimes very pale, almost white flowers. Its form *variegata* is more handsome as the leaves have broad creamy-white edges. Another fine variegated hebe is *H.* × *andersonii variegata*, eventually 4–5 feet tall, but often seen at about a foot, used for foliage effect in summer bedding in public parks, especially in coastal towns.

These hebes make few demands on the soil, growing well in quite poor kinds and those containing much chalk. They stand up well to salt-laden winds.

Hebe elliptica is a good hedging shrub.

The variety Midsummer Beauty bears hundreds of long spikes of lavender flowers throughout the summer and early autumn.

The colourful Sun Roses grow well on dry sunny banks or rockeries.

Helianthemum

The Sun Roses are charming little plants, that are very useful for many places in the garden, but practically indispensable for helping to clothe dry, sunny banks or, because they grow a mere 9 inches or so tall, for planting in sunny pockets on the rock garden.

H. nummularium (*H. chamaecistus*) is a native plant that has inch-wide yellow flowers. The many hybrids and varieties are very popular indeed, especially as they are easy to grow and have a wide colour range. Named kinds include 'Ben Afflick' which has orange and buff flowers,

'Firedragon' with crimson, 'Marigold', double yellow and 'Rose of Leeswood' with double flowers of a soft pink. There is a white variety called 'The Bride' and, in contrast, 'Henfield Brilliant' is brick red. There are many others, of which some have grey or silvery-grey leaves.

Left to themselves these plants are inclined to become straggly, but this can generally be overcome by hard pruning after flowering is over, usually in late July. This is not necessary merely for the sake of tidiness, but will encourage new flowering growth to appear. Sometimes this summer pruning may even cause the plants to produce more flowers in the autumn.

These shrubs do well in poor, but well-drained soils and their only real requirement is a sunny place, where they will produce their flowers freely without much attention. They dislike cold, wet soils.

A variety of *Helianthemum nummularium* has inch-wide pink flowers.

Hibiscus

Hibiscus syriacus and its numerous varieties, sometimes known as Tree Hollyhocks, are invaluable shrubs for they flower late, when a good many shrubs are already over. They begin to flower in July and it is sometimes October before the last flowers appear. The flowers are trumpet-shaped, much like those of the popular hollyhocks to which they are related, and there is now a fair colour range. These plants grow slowly to about 6–8 feet, making upright, rather than spreading bushes. They will grow in any reasonable garden soil but must have a sunny position. Dead wood should be removed when the plants are well in leaf which may not be until May.

Apart from the late-summer flowering, two of these shrubs at least are useful in that they have blue flowers. These are 'Blue Bird' and 'Coeleste'. *H. syriacus coeruleus plenus* has double purplish-blue flowers, *roseus plenus* has double lilac-red flowers and *violaceus plenus* double reddish-purple. 'Hamabo', a popular kind, has pale pink blooms with a crimson blotch at the petal bases and often with pink-tipped petals. 'Duc de Brabant' is a double red and *monstrosus plenus* a double white, purplish at the centre.

Hibiscus syriacus Coeleste has blue flowers in late summer.

The Woodbridge variety is rose-pink with maroon blotches.

Hydrangea petiolaris

Hydrangea

Most people think of hydrangeas as the shrubs with large mop-heads of flowers, in blue or pink, often seen at their best in the gardens of seaside towns in late summer. These, the 'hortensia' varieties of *H. macrophylla,* are deservedly popular, as they flower well, look spectacular when in bloom and are not difficult to grow, succeeding in sun or semi-shade. On chalk or lime the flowers are pink or red and the colours are so pleasant that it is hardly worth going to the considerable trouble of trying to make them blue by adding 'blueing' powder or aluminium sulphate to the soil in considerable quantities at frequent intervals. On acid soils the flowers are blue while on neutral soils they may be either or both on the same shrub and, in fact, this may happen on fairly deep soils overlying chalk. There are a number of named varieties, in shades of pink and red, not all of them guaranteed to blue. There are also one or two white-flowered varieties.

A variation is the 'Lace-cap' hydrangea, with flat heads of flowers, large sterile florets surrounding small fertile florets. 'Blue Wave' is a fine variety and 'Lanarth White' always attracts attention.

These varieties of *H. macrophylla* are not the only hydrangeas. Among the other hardier kinds are *H. paniculata grandiflora,* with cone-shaped spikes of white flowers and

H. arborescens grandiflora, which has large heads of white flowers. *H. quercifolia*, the Oak-leaved Hydrangea, is not quite so hardy but has attractive leaves that turn bright colours in autumn.

Different in habit from all these, is *H. petiolaris*, the Climbing Hydrangea, a self-clinging climber, a most unusual plant for a wall of any aspect, or for growing up a tree.

Hydrangeas must have a moisture retaining soil otherwise the shrubs will flag noticeably in dry periods and look very sorry for themselves. Even then it may be necessary to give them a really thorough watering in periods of drought.

Pruning, where necessary, is done in April and consists of cutting away weak growths and frost-damaged wood.

Hydrangea macrophylla (left) and a Lace-cap variety (*right*).

The Hidcote hybrid of Hypericum (*left*) and *Hypericum calycinum* (*below*).

Hypericum

Hypericum calycinum, usually referred to as Rose of Sharon, and often looked upon as almost a weed, is a useful plant for clothing dry banks, for those places under trees and shrubs where little else will grow, or for the tops of double walls. Its bright yellow flowers, with a big brush of stamens in the centre, are a familiar sight in many gardens and in railway cuttings in the chalk of the southern counties.

There are better, much more aristocratic kinds than this, however, fully worthy of a place of honour in the garden. The hybrid 'Hidcote', for instance, bears large, saucer-shaped flowers freely from July to autumn and grows to 5–6 feet tall. 'Rowallane Hybrid' is somewhat better as it easily reaches 6 feet in the milder counties and has flowers that may be 3 inches across. Unfortunately it is not hardy enough for the open garden except in warmer places and elsewhere it needs the shelter of a wall or a protected site.

Other good kinds include 'Elstead Variety', about 4 feet tall, *patulum henryi,* 3–4 feet, with good autumn leaf colour, and *patulum grandiflorum,* about 3 feet tall. In addition there are several dwarfer forms suitable for the rock garden, ranging from the 6 inches of *H. polyphyllum* to the 18 inches of *H. kalmianum.*

All these shrubs are sun-lovers and they do well in hot, dry situations, particularly on the chalk. *H. calycinum,* an evergreen, should be trimmed over with shears. 'Hidcote' and 'Rowallane Hybrid' may be hard pruned in spring but others need little attention except for the removal of dead wood.

This is a useful plant for dry banks

Jasminum nudiflorum will provide colour every winter without fail.

Jasminum

Winter flowers are always welcome, particularly if they are produced unfailingly, whatever the weather. The Winter Jasmine, *Jasminum nudiflorum* can always be guaranteed to open its bright yellow flowers on the leafless stems, even in hard frost or when deep snow covers the ground, unless pruning has been neglected. The flowers are produced on young growths made the previous year so that after flowering is over some thinning out of older shoots is needed, otherwise in a very few years, the bush will make a mass of tangled growths and flowering will be diminished. Specimens are normally grown against walls or fences, of any aspect, or may be trained over pergolas or arches. They may reach 12–15 feet in height.

The Summer Jessamine *J. officinale* is also a plant for a wall, though it should be a sunny one. Its white, sweetly fragrant flowers appear from June onwards into early autumn. It produces long twining growths and, properly trained, can cover a house side. Regular pruning is unnecessary, but it does pay to carry out some thinning out of shoots every two or three years, otherwise the growth is so vigorous that it will make a tangled mass several feet thick.

A hybrid between the Summer Jasmine and *J. beesianum* is *J. stephanense,* which is almost as vigorous and bears sweet-scented pale pink flowers in June and July. Like its parent it needs a sunny wall. Otherwise, like the others described here, it will grow in any normal garden soil.

Flowers of *Jasminum officinale* the fragrant summer species (*below*) and in shrub form (*left*).

Kalmia

Allied to the rhododendrons and belonging to the same family as the heathers (*Ericaceae*), the Kalmias need a lime-free, preferably peaty soil. In its native America *K. latifolia,* the most commonly grown species is known as the Mountain Laurel and its bright pink flowers make the mountains of the Eastern States very colourful in May and June. There it grows to 25–30 feet, although in Britain it seldom exceeds about 8–10 feet, but is well worth growing where the soil is

suitable. No pruning is needed, but, as with rhododendrons, it is worth removing dead flowers.

K. angustifolia, the Sheep Laurel, is a good deal less tall, reaching at the most 3 feet and usually less. It has narrow leaves and rosy-red flowers. An even more dwarf form is *K. polifolia,* about a foot or so in height, flowering earlier than the others, its purplish flowers opening in April.

All these kalmias prefer semi-shade and moist, though not perpetually boggy, soil. Peat and leafmould dug in at planting time and also used subsequently as a surface mulch, will do much to create the right conditions.

Kalmia latifolia has evergreen leaves like those of rhododendrons and the flowers are borne in clusters at the end of the stems. These are attractive in bud, looking like pink boxes, opening to bell-shaped blossoms.

Kerria

There is one species only of Kerria, *K. japonica,* although there are several varieties of it. One does not often see *K. japonica* itself, as most people prefer to grow the larger double-flowered form, *pleniflora* (or *flore-plena*) which makes a considerably larger plant. Yet the ordinary kind has its merits. It grows about 5–6 feet tall when planted against a wall or fence of any aspect, not quite so tall when grown in the open. It makes a clump of green stems, somewhat arching in habit, on which, mainly in April and May but also at other times of the year, appear numerous orange-yellow flowers, not unlike small single roses or large buttercups.

There is also a dwarf form, *picta* (or *variegata*), which has leaves edged with silvery-white.

Any kind of soil seems suitable for this shrub provided it is not too poor and dry. If it is to be planted in the open, a reasonably sheltered position should be chosen and it does not matter if this is in semi-shade. Pruning is not generally required. However, as plants make fairly extensive thickets it is worth thinning out the stems occasionally to let in light and air.

Kerria japonica pleniflora is the variety generally cultivated and often trained against a wall (*left*). It has large two-inch double flowers and grows to about eight feet with stiff upright stems.

The hybrid *Laburnum × vossii* is more upright and tree-like in growth.

Laburnum

The laburnums are strictly small trees, but they never grow very tall and although they may be grown as standards on a single stem, often fork low down, giving the appearance of a tall shrub. They grow quite quickly, but rarely to more than 20 feet in height and it is more usual to see them at about 15 feet. The common laburnum (*L. anagyroides*) is pleasant enough in late May and June with its trails of golden flowers, and it does well near the sea and in exposed, windy gardens. It is not, however, as good as the hybrid, *L. × vossii,* which has longer trails of flowers, some 15–18 inches in length, borne a little later. This kind also has the advantage of

producing fewer of the poisonous black seeds that make some gardeners with small children reluctant to plant the beautiful laburnums.

Another kind which flowers later than the ordinary laburnum is its variety *autumnale* and with this, too, the flower trails are longer.

Laburnums grow in any kind of soil, including those containing much chalk. They do not require pruning, but, where there are small children about it is advisable to go over the trees after flowering and cut off the dead flower trails to prevent the seed from setting.

Lavandula

One of the most pleasant ways of growing that old garden favourite, the lavender, is to use it as a hedge, either as a low boundary hedge or an internal hedge to divide one part of the garden from another. Lavenders, with their ever-grey leaves, associate well with other silvery or grey-leaved plants in the shrub or herbaceous border. A few separate plants in a broad paved area, planted in the space gained by removing a flagstone, looks very effective.

L. spica is the Old English Lavender and there are several forms of it, of which 'Grappenhall Variety' at about 3 feet, sometimes reaching 4 feet, is the tallest and 'Beechwood Blue' at less than 1 foot is about the shortest. This kind has flowers of a good blue and there are others such as *rosea* with pink flowers and 'Twickel Purple' with deep purple blooms, as well as several other dwarfs at about 15 inches. These dwarfs are particularly useful in very small gardens where the bigger kinds would look out of place.

Any well-drained soil and sunny position suits the lavenders and it is all the better if the soil is really well-drained and on the dry side in summer. Apart from the pruning the plants get when the stems are cut for drying or decoration it is as well to trim them over in April, avoiding cutting into the old wood.

The many varieties of *Lavandula spica* look very attractive as internal hedges flanking a pathway. They should be planted at least $1\frac{1}{2}$ feet from the edge to allow for development without impeding progress along the path.

Lonicera

The loniceras are the Honeysuckles and the native *L. periclymenum* is also known as the Woodbine. This has a couple of varieties, more often planted in gardens than the wild kind and both deserving a place because they follow each other in flower, giving a continuous display between them from May to October. The Early Dutch Honeysuckle, *L. periclymenum belgica,* with reddish-purple flowers, starts the season in late spring, and the Late Dutch, *L. p. serotina,* with somewhat richer coloured flowers, carries it into the autumn.

There are numerous others, however, some more vigorous, some lacking the delicious fragrance one associates with

Lonicera periclymenum is native to Britain and selected varieties are easy to cultivate, especially over garden arches (*right*).

these plants, but with larger flowers. One of the finest is the hybrid, *L.* × *americana,* which is extremely free-flowering with large flowers opening white but ageing to deep yellow, in big clusters in June or July. They lack fragrance but the plant is worth growing for the speed with which it covers a pergola, fence or other support.

The native Woodbine flourishes on heavy clay soils and all loniceras do well in shade, although they will not object to sunnier situations. The twiners need some support for their growths and often look well if they are allowed to scramble through other shrubs or into trees. They need pruning only if they become too vigorous, when it is sufficient to shorten the strongest shoots in autumn.

Lupinus

The lupins that are most well known are the hardy herbaceous perennials, especially the Russell lupins in a wide colour range. But there is a fine shrub, popularly known as the Tree Lupin, which has very similar flowers, although the spikes are shorter at about 9 inches long. This is *Lupinus arboreus,* an excellent shrub for dry soils, for hot sunny banks and for poor, stony soils that sometimes present problems. In fact it does better on these soils than on richer, moisture-retaining kinds, which is understandable, as it originated in California.

Its maximum height is about 6 feet, but in most places it rarely seems to exceed 4–5 feet. So rapidly does it grow, however, that it can attain its eventual height in no more than two or three years. Its sweetly fragrant flowers are produced throughout most of June and July. Normally they are a fairly bright yellow, but there are various named colour forms available including the deep yellow 'Golden Spire' and 'Yellow Boy', 'Mauve Queen', rosy-mauve, and the pure white 'Snow Queen'. Plants are easily raised from seed and other colour forms may appear among the seedlings.

There is no need to prune this shrub, though it is worth deadheading it to conserve its strength. It does not like being transplanted so that it is best to plant out from pots.

Lupinus arboreus is an excellent shrub for dry soils.

The Tree Lupins make shrubby plants that develop sweetly fragrant flowers in June.

Magnolia

The magnolias are among the most beautiful of all shrubs, though they are not planted as widely as they might be because they have a reputation for being 'difficult' and because, generally, they are slow growing. Several, however, are reasonably easy to grow provided they are given the right soil and, if carefully planted, some flower very early in life. Certainly not the least beautiful is *M. stellata*, which produces starry flowers with drooping white petals. Plants a mere 18 inches tall will start to flower the year following planting.

Magnolia stellata produces starry white flowers in March and April.

M. soulangeana is no more difficult to grow and also flowers early in life. It has a number of varieties but *lennei* is the best. In June this produces flowers that look much like large tulips, purplish-rose on the outside, white inside.

By contrast, *M. grandiflora*, a wall evergreen, may take many years to flower, unless 'Exmouth Variety' or 'Goliath', two kinds that flower much younger, are planted. This, one of the most magnificent of all magnolias, flowers in late summer producing enormous fragrant creamy flowers, 9–10 inches across. It may grow to 30 feet, with a proportionate spread.

These magnolias do not mind chalky soils, provided they

are not thin and deep, well-cultivated alkaline soil is probably preferable to a hot, dry sandy acid soil. Before planting the opportunity should be taken to incorporate moist peat and leafmould in lavish quantities and it is worth lightening heavier clay soils with sharp sand in addition. An annual mulch in spring with moist peat and leafmould, or rotted garden compost is always beneficial to magnolias. They require no pruning, apart from the removal of any dead wood, but they must have plenty of water during droughts, particularly when young. When planting great care should be taken not to damage the roots.

Magnolia soulangeana (above) with outline of the shrub form (*left*) is one of the commonly grown deciduous species.

Mahonia aquifolium is an excellent shrub for shady conditions but will grow in more open situations (*right*).

Mahonia

Related to the berberis and sometimes included under berberis in catalogues, these evergreen shrubs differ mainly in having large leathery leaves divided into a number of leaflets. The kind mainly grown is *M. aquifolium,* an excellent shrub for under the shade of trees though it will grow in more open situations, in time reaching some 3–6 feet tall, with a spread of 3–5 feet. The large leaves have up to seven pairs of spiny toothed leaflets. As winter approaches these turn purplish or are often flushed or edged with red. These colours persist until the spring. In late winter the shrub flowers, producing lemon-yellow deliciously fragrant blooms, in long clusters, springing from a central point. The flowers are followed by berries, green at first, changing to dark purple with a plum-like bloom, almost as handsome as the flowers. The shrub spreads by underground suckers, but seldom at a rate to make it a nuisance and this habit makes it useful for ground cover under trees. It also makes it easy to propagate by digging up pieces of sucker growth.

M. japonica is a taller plant, with even more fragrant flowers, with a distinct lily-of-the-valley scent. These are produced in late winter in longer clusters or sprays.

These mahonias are not demanding in their soil requirements. The leafy soil beneath trees suits them admirably though they will flourish in any kind of garden soil including chalky ones.

The hybrid *Malus* × *purpurea* in flower

Malus

These are the crab-apples and, like several other plants mentioned in this book, they are small trees rather than shrubs. They are grown for their flowers as much as for their richly coloured fruits and some provide an added bonus when their leaves turn bright colours in autumn, before falling. Some, indeed, have purplish coppery leaves throughout. One with this characteristic is *M.* × *eleyi,* which grows to about 20 feet tall, with rosy-crimson flowers in late April and early May, followed by masses of small purplish crabs. *M.* × *purpurea* is another fine hybrid that has purplish leaves and reddish crimson flowers, produced rather earlier than those of *M.* × *eleyi*.

Malus × purpurea

John Downie (*right*) is planted chiefly for its large fruit.

'John Downie' is the kind planted more than any other, for the sake of its large scarlet and yellow fruits that follow the white flowers. 'Dartmouth Crab', another white-flowered kind, crops heavily, its fruits crimson with a bluish plum-bloom. The yellow-fruited kinds such as 'Golden Hornet' are unusually handsome, though their fruits are smaller. There are also several kinds with double flowers, including 'Katherine', pink at first, ageing to white, with red fruits.

These Crabs will grow in all kinds of soil, particularly those containing lime, preferably in open, sunny positions. Pruning is unnecessary except for shape or to restrict over-lush growth.

Olearia

The olearias are the Daisy Bushes, natives of Australia and New Zealand, evergreen shrubs, many of them tender, though suitable for coastal gardens in the milder counties. Though not fully hardy, *O. haastii* is hardy enough to be grown successfully in quite cold northern gardens, where one can see old specimens, 4–5 feet tall, bearing numerous clusters of small white daisy flowers in late summer. It makes an unusual and informal evergreen hedge.

In warmer gardens near the coast, even in the south-east, provided it is planted there in a sheltered place, the hybrid *O.* × *scilloniensis* will put up a good show. Its flowers are much larger and a well-grown bush, 3–5 feet tall, is a handsome sight when it flowers in May and early June. Even when out of flower it is attractive for its leaves are a good grey-green. In somewhat milder but exposed seaside areas, it is possible to grow *O. gunniana,* the Tasmanian Daisy Bush, which again flowers in May and June, white in the species, but also available with flowers that are rosy-pink, blue or lavender in colour.

These Daisy Bushes will grow in any normal garden soil and do not object to slight shade. A trim with shears after they have flowered will improve their appearance. If they become leggy and gaunt they may be pruned quite hard.

Olearia gunniana

Olearia × scilloniensis is a hybrid that has larger than average flowers in May and June.

Paeonia

The shrubby paeonies, varieties of *P. suffruticosa*, known as Moutan paeonies, are among the most showy of garden plants for a few weeks in April and May. Their large semi-double or fully double flowers in shades of crimson, pink, carmine, purple and white, often splashed with another colour, are among the glories of the garden at that time. They grow to 4–6 feet tall and a well-grown plant may be 3–4 feet wide. They are not difficult plants to grow but, although hardy, they may be damaged by frosts and for that reason are best planted in sheltered situations, particularly where the morning sun cannot reach them, because rapid evaporation of dew or frost will damage the delicate blooms. They will grow in any reasonably rich and well-dug soil.

The single, deep crimson flowers of *P. delavayi* which is a 5 feet tall Chinese species will always attract attention. A very good effect can also be obtained with the large bright yellow single blooms of *P. lutea* of which the best form is *ludlowii*. This variety should reach 6 feet with ease. *P. lutea* has been crossed with *P. suffruticosa* to produce the *lemoinei* hybrids, such as 'Alice Harding', a double canary yellow, and 'Souvenir de Maxine Cornu', which has very large bright yellow flowers and petals edged with red.

These tree paeonies need no pruning but dead wood should be cut away in the spring.

The colourful flowers of the paeonies always attract attention during the flowering period of May and June.

The Mock Orange variety, Sybille, has richly scented flowers and reaches 5 feet in height.

Philadelphus

These are the well-loved Mock Oranges, known to most gardeners for the scent of their early summer flowers, although not all of them have the piercingly sweet 'orange-blossom' fragrance of the old-fashioned, commonly grown *P. coronarius* with its creamy-white flowers. This may grow to 10 feet tall, producing annually a mass of young shoots, either springing from the base or from the older wood, and it is on this young growth that the Mock Oranges produce most of their flowers, which gives the clue to pruning. This consists in thinning out some of the oldest stems each year, after the flowers have faded, thus giving the younger growth a better chance to ripen. These young growths are always paler in colour so that it is an easy matter to differentiate when pruning.

There is a particularly beautiful variety of *P. coronarius,* known as *aureus,* with golden-yellow leaves which, after midsummer, turn greenish-yellow. In spring it is an outstanding sight.

The Mock Oranges are easy plants to grow but prefer a sunny position. The old vernacular name 'Syringa' still persists, although the true syringas are the lilacs.

Philadelphus coronarius is the old-fashioned, commonly grown, form.

Pieris

Double value shrubs are usually worth growing and anyone with a lime-free soil, of the type on which rhododendrons thrive, should grow pieris. If there is room for one only it should be *P. forrestii* (*P. formosa forrestii*) in one of its finest forms, such as 'Exbury Form' or 'Wakehurst Variety'. The great glory of this evergreen shrub is in the spring or early summer, when the young growths are developing. These bear a resemblance to shuttlecocks on the ends of the branches, are brilliant red and remain so for some weeks before turning a light green, which turns darker as the summer advances. Sprays of white, fragrant flowers similar to lily-of-the-valley appear in April and May when the red young growths are at their best.

Pieris forrestii, sometimes known as *Pieris formosa forrestii*

The shrub will reach 10 feet in milder places, with a proportionate spread. In less protected places a height of about 6 feet is more usual. In general, pruning is unnecessary, except to remove dead or dying wood.

Where space allows, other species of pieris may be grown. *P. floribunda*, for instance, does not take up much room, as it usually grows only to about 4 feet and is, in any case, a slow-grower. *P. japonica,* which ultimately grows to about 10 feet, has larger flowers that are produced in March and April, a little earlier than other species. Another of these plants, is *P. taiwanensis*, which reaches the same height and flowers freely during April and May. None, however, has quite the attraction of the best forms of *P. forrestii*.

This shrub will reach 10 feet in mild situations.

Potentilla

These are the Shrubby Cinquefoils, mostly varieties of *P. fruticosa*, a deciduous shrub about 4 feet tall, although its named forms range in height from 1 foot upwards to over 4 feet. They flower over a very long period, usually from June to September, or even later into the autumn and are invaluable from this point of view alone. In the species itself the flowers are yellow, but there are many subtle shades of this colour and in the varieties it is possible to find pale primrose as in, 'Katherine Dykes', one of the best of all, reaching 4 feet, canary yellow, as in 'Elizabeth', $2\frac{1}{2}$ feet tall, and golden-yellow, in such varieties as *farreri*.

Potentilla fruticosa is invaluable because it flowers from June until late autumn.

This variety grows to 2 feet and comes into flower earlier than the others. A coppery yellow, or orange, can be obtained with the 'Tangerine' variety and a creamy-yellow with *vilmoriniana*. This is an excellent variety because its silvery, almost white leaves add to its attraction. Apart from these there are white-flowered kinds, of which the 1 foot tall *mandschurica,* with grey leaves, is one of the best.

Although the potentillas do best in sunny, open positions, they will tolerate a little shade and the quality of soil appears to be immaterial. They do not require pruning. Those of more upright growth may be used to make pleasant internal hedges, flowering as they do over such a long period.

Prunus

This is a big genus containing the almonds, apricots, cherries, peaches, plums, sloes and related fruits, as well as a wide range of ornamentals, principally the Japanese flowering cherries. It also includes various hedging plants such as laurels and myrobalan plums, some of which, like *P. × cistena,* are becoming increasingly popular for making coloured-leaf hedges.

As there are some two hundred or more prunus in cultivation the choice can be somewhat bewildering. For sheer colour in spring there is nothing to beat the hybrid Japanese cherries, although they need choosing with care as some grow too large for small gardens. For really confined spaces there is 'Amanogawa', in growth like a Lombardy Poplar, with fragrant, semi-double pink flowers. Small, too, is 'Kiku Shidare Zakura', also known as 'Cheal's Weeping Cherry', with arching shoots bearing fully double, deep pink flowers. Larger, with wide-spread branches, is 'Kanzan', with deep pink, double flowers, very freely borne. There are many

(*From left to right*) Cherry Laurel, Flowering Almond, Japanese Cherry and Purple Cherry.

others, in pinks pale and deep, and some good white-flowered kinds.

P. subhirtella autumnalis, a small tree, is popular because it produces its white, single or semi-double flowers from November onwards, particularly when the weather is mild.

More shrubby in growth is *P. triloba multiplex,* a dwarf almond, which grows to about 6 feet tall, or more against a wall, and has delightful rosy-pink, 'bachelor's button' flowers in March and April.

P. cerasifera atropurpurea (*pissardii*) is the Purple-leaved Plum, a decorative small tree, also used for hedging. *P. c. nigra* has darker, almost black leaves and pink flowers.

An attractive bush is made by the dwarf almond, *P. amygdalus tenella* 'Fire Hill', which grows to 4 feet with a similar spread and in April bears many rosy-crimson flowers.

All the prunus do well on chalk. Little pruning is required for trees and shrubs in the open but those against walls require pruning and training to keep their shape.

Pyracantha coccinea lalandii is a delightful wall-trained shrub with orange-red fruit.

Pyracantha

Seen more often as wall-trained shrubs rather than in the open, pyracanthas or Firethorns are notable for their freely produced colourful berries that follow the pretty clusters of white flowers, much like those of our native hawthorn. Against walls these plants will grow to 10–20 feet but in the open, where they may be used as hedges or as specimen plants, they are a good deal less tall. They will grow in sun or shade, do well on north walls, and do not have any special soil requirements, growing well on those containing much chalk.

Berry colours range from bright crimson, through orange to yellow. One of the best of the crimson-fruited kinds is the tall-growing *P. atalantoides* (*P. gibbsii*), which also has a fine yellow-berried form *aurea*. In *P. coccinea* the fruits are orange-red and it is the variety of this known as *lalandii,* with larger berries of a similar colour, that is the most popular pyracantha. However, orange is not everyone's colour and those who prefer something quieter may like to plant *P. crenulata flava,* which has bright yellow fruits.

Against walls these shrubs need pruning occasionally as they grow vigorously and long growths can become a nuisance. In the open little attention is necessary. Pruning is best undertaken wearing gloves as the aptly-named firethorns are indeed thorny.

Rhododendron

This is a large and bewildering genus, particularly as it includes the azaleas. It contains a vast range of plants, both deciduous and evergreen, in a wonderful colour range, varying in height from less than 1 foot to the 20–30 feet of some tree-like species grown in the milder counties. Most kinds are hardy outdoors anywhere in the British Isles, some can only be grown properly in warmer places while some need the protection of a cool greenhouse.

Although the normal flowering period is April and May there are some which come into flower earlier than this, while others delay their flowering until June or July, so that the rhododendron season is not as short as may be supposed.

The Princess Morika variety of the Rhododendrons (*left*) and *R. azalea mollis* (*right*).

R. yakusimanum (*left*) and *R. augustinii*

However diverse these shrubs may be, they have, with one or two minor exceptions, one thing in common and that is their dislike of lime or chalk in the soil or even in the water that may be used to water them. Acid woodland soils, those containing much leafmould or peat, in lime-free districts suit them best.

It is possible to mention here a few kinds only from the very many available. The Hardy Hybrids are among the best for the normal garden. They include such kinds as the old favourites 'Pink Pearl', the rosy-carmine 'Cynthia', 'Handsworth Scarlet', 'Gomer Waterer', blush-pink, and many others, some with handsome darker blotches on their petals.

Among the species *R. augustinii* with blue flowers is outstanding and *R. repens* is a fine prostrate kind for woodland ground cover, with scarlet flowers. *R. impeditum,* mauve, *R. calostrum,* pink to mauve, and *R. hanceanum nanum,* yellow, are all dome-shaped plants good as rock garden shrubs.

The Kurume hybrids are among the best of the evergreen azaleas, with many good colours. The *mollis* hybrids, 4–5 feet tall, with large flowers are excellent deciduous azaleas.

Rhus

The rhus most commonly seen in gardens is *R. typhina*, the well-known Stag's Horn Sumach. It will grow anywhere, but has a bad habit of sending up suckers yards away, so be warned. For this reason it is not a good specimen for a lawn, although it is often seen in this situation. It usually grows 12–15 feet tall, so needs a fair amount of space.

By far the best of the rhus is *R. cotinus*, correctly known nowadays as *Cotinus coggygria,* but described here as it is still found under Rhus in many catalogues. This is the Smoke Tree, Wig Tree or Venetian Sumach, although the latter name is hardly ever heard. Smoke Tree and Wig Tree are much more appropriate names as when it is in flower the flower-stems, many of them flowerless, are so slender that it looks as though the shrub is wearing a huge pale pink wig. In autumn these fine stems turn grey and one can see why the name Smoke Tree has been given to this shrub.

This is another plant for a poor soil, otherwise it may not flower freely, but will produce too much foliage. On the other hand the variety known as *atropurpurea foliis purpureis* 'Notcutt's Variety' might be given better treatment, as the main attraction lies in the deep maroon leaves.

These are good plants for the busy or lazy gardener as no pruning is needed except to remove dead wood or any branches that spoil the shape.

The crimson spikes of *Rhus typhina* are a common sight in late summer and the leaves turn scarlet before they fall.

Ribes sanguineum, known as the Flowering Currant, is one of the easiest shrubs to grow in any soil in a sunny position.

Ribes

Most gardeners know the Flowering Currant, *Ribes sanguineum*, one of the easiest of plants to grow in any soil and sunny situation, although it is not the most aristocratic of shrubs. The species itself has rosy-pink flowers in March and April but the pink is not a very good colour. There are several good red-flowered cultivars, however, such as 'King Edward VII' which is deep crimson, and 'Pulborough

Scarlet', as well as an unusual one, *brocklebankii,* with golden leaves and pink flowers. All these reach from 6–10 feet in height and benefit from hard pruning after the flowers are over. The shoots that have flowered may then be cut out or cut back as required.

There are other ornamental currants worthy of a more prominent position. The Buffalo Currant or Golden Currant *R. aureum* (*R. odoratum*) has short trails of sweetly-scented yellow flowers in spring. It grows to about 6–8 feet tall and its leaves turn a good yellow in autumn. *R.* × *gordonianum,* a hybrid between the two species described above, has bronze-red and yellow flowers and red autumn leaves. The Fuchsia-flowered Gooseberry, *R. speciosum,* is an evergreen and belongs to the gooseberry side of the genus. It makes a good wall shrub, with drooping red fuchsia-like flowers.

This shrub should be planted from October to March. *R. speciosum* will sometimes suffer from frost damage but the other species are quite hardy. All the varieties of this shrub can be increased by taking cuttings of the firm young stems. These should be between 6–8 inches in length, and can be inserted in ordinary soil outdoors during October. Most cuttings treated in this way should root satisfactorily by the following spring.

R. aureum has sweetly-scented yellow flowers.

Rosa

Roses, in all their varied forms and colours, are among the aristocrats of flowering shrubs. Few shrubs come into flower in June and continue flowering until October or later, as the modern hybrid tea and floribunda roses do.

There are roses for practically all purposes and no other shrub is so diverse in its flower colour. In the hybrid teas and floribundas, pinks, reds and yellows predominate, with a few good white varieties and, in recent years, a good many on the orange or vermilion side of red have been introduced, with a few others verging on lilac. In the older roses it is possible to find purples, maroons, magentas, and mauves as well as the deepest crimsons and delicate pinks. There are the striped roses such as 'Rosa Mundi' and partly-coloured varieties such as 'York and Lancaster', grown for over four centuries, with its petals sometimes pink and sometimes almost white, usually with both kinds on the same flower.

Among these 'old' roses, are the most heavily fragrant kinds, their scent quite unlike the light fragrance of most of the modern roses. Many have a short flowering period, around midsummer, but others have recurrent or 'perpetual' flowers. In contrast *R. rubrifolia* is grown for its purple leaves.

In this short space it is impossible to mention further names, particularly as new varieties of hybrid teas, floribundas and even shrub roses, appear annually. There are many suppliers of fine hybrid teas and floribundas in the country and it would be invidious to recommend particular nurseries. There are, however, few nurseries that have a really wide range of 'old' roses, Bourbons, hybrid musks, hybrid perpetuals, China roses, and species roses. The widest selection is held by Sunningdale Nurseries, Windlesham, Surrey, an establishment that is well worth a visit around midsummer or during late June, when most of these roses are in bloom.

The Rose Garden – still as popular as ever it was.

Roses will do well on clay soils provided they are properly cultivated, just as they will flourish on most soils except the very thin ones overlying chalk, which provide the most difficult conditions for most shrubs. Mulching in spring is necessary to keep them growing vigorously.

Hybrid teas and floribundas are usually pruned in late March. For ordinary garden display hard pruning is not necessary and reducing stems by about a third or a half their length, cutting back to above an outward-pointing bud, is usually sufficient, cutting out thin growths at the same time and endeavouring to keep the centre of the bush open.

Rambler roses are pruned immediately after they have flowered, cutting away the old flowered shoots. Climbing hybrid teas are pruned by thinning out some of the old flowered shoots once the blooms are over; the plants are gone over again in April to cut off dead growth and thin, weakly shoots and tipping back the ends of unripened shoots.

Little pruning is required for the 'old' roses. Some of the oldest stems can be cut away each year after flowering and the longest growths are shortened by one third in February or March.

The species roses also need little pruning, though when bushes become overgrown it is necessary to cut out the oldest shoots and thin growth, to encourage the production of new, strong shoots on which the best flowers are produced.

Flowers and fruit of *Rosa moyesii*

A. Mrs Pierre S. Dupont
B. Ellen Poulsen
C. *R. mundi*
D. Hips of a species rose
E. Masquerade
F. Constance Spry

Rubus

The Brambles are grown for their flowers, their fruits, or their white stems. Some are valuable for shady places or rough banks. Of the twenty or more kinds in cultivation, pride of place as far as flowers go must be given to the hybrid, 'Tridel', because of its shining, paper-white flowers, with a central mass of yellow stamens, looking not unlike single roses. These are freely borne in April and May, on arching shoots which may reach 9–10 feet in length.

Of the white-stemmed kinds, *R. cockburnianus* and *R. thibetanus* are about the best. They are seen at their best in winter when the leaves are off and the ghostly-white stems can be appreciated.

Rubus thibetanus has white stems and is at its best in winter.

An unusual kind is *R. ulmifolius bellidiflorus,* which makes a wide spreading clump in a wild garden or may be trained back against a wall, or over a pergola or fence. It has double pink flowers in July and August.

All these shrubs can be grown in any kind of soil and may either be cut hard back to keep them within bounds, or be left to grow at will, merely cutting out the oldest wood each spring. The white-stemmed kinds look more attractive if they are pruned hard each spring so as to encourage the formation of new stems.

The best ornamental Rubus is Tridel, a hybrid from *R. delicosus* and *R. trilobus*

Senecio

There are not many daisy-flowered shrubs available for the garden and this genus includes 1,300 species, very few of garden value. The senecio usually grown in gardens, referred to as either *S. greyi* or *S. laxifolius,* is probably neither of these species, but a hybrid. It attracts attention not only because of its bright yellow daisies, but also because of the silvery grey appearance of its young leaves, which makes them look as though they are covered with felt. In older leaves the greyness is confined to the edges. Underneath the leaves are white.

Fine specimens of this plant, up to 3–4 feet tall, are to be seen in gardens near the sea round most of the coast, for this shrub will tolerate well the wind and salt sea spray. However, it grows well inland, provided it can be given a fairly sheltered position in full sunlight. It is also a useful plant for the chalk garden. Gardeners who plant mainly for

Senecio laxifolius is one of the few daisy-flowered shrubs available.

the foliage effect often remove the flower-heads before they open to preserve the grey-white appearance of the plant, but most people generally prefer to let the handsome yellow daisies develop fully. Little pruning is needed, although after severe winters there may be a fair amount of dead growth to be cut away.

There are many other senecios available, although they are not often seen. *S. compactus* is very much like the plant that has been described above, except that it does not exceed 3 feet in height and is usually considerably less, and both its leaves and flowers are smaller. *S. elaeagnifolius* grows to about 4 feet in height and is much denser and more stiff in habit. Both this and the taller *S. hectori,* which has white centres and white petals to the flowers, are really only suitable for seaside planting in milder areas such as the south-west and the west of Britain.

Sorbus aucuparia is valued for its orange-red fruits, copiously produced in autumn.

Sorbus

The Mountain Ash or Rowan (*Sorbus aucuparia*), a native plant, will, in time, reach 20–30 feet, making a round-headed tree, so its position should be chosen with some care. The leaves, divided into many narrow leaflets, are graceful, and the small white flowers are produced in clusters in May.

Although this is among the best of small trees, it does have the disadvantage that the fruits seldom stay long enough for them to be fully appreciated for they are eagerly devoured by birds. Fortunately there is a yellow-fruited form, *xanthocarpa,* which is less attractive to birds. There are other forms, too, including *asplenifolia,* with deeply-cut, fern-like leaves, and *fastigiata,* more upright in growth and thus more suitable for restricted spaces.

There are many other sorbuses and among these *S. discolor* is worth growing for its bright red, long-lasting autumn foliage. *S. hupehensis,* somewhat taller, attracts attention because of its white or pale pink fruits. *S. essertauiana,* 20–25 feet, carries great clusters of rather small scarlet fruits which hang on the leafless trees well into winter.

Sorbus hupehensis

(*Above*) Fruit and flowers of *Sorbus aucuparia*

Spartium

The only species here is *S. junceum,* the Spanish Broom, familiar to many gardeners. It is an attractive shrub but peculiar because it is almost leafless, with green, rush-like stems. The species name *junceum* acknowledges the similarity to the rushes, called *Juncus*. The real attraction lies in the large yellow pea flowers that are borne all summer. These are worth cutting to bring indoors for the sake of the scent of lilies that they exhale.

S. junceum thrives best in poor, dry, stony soils and is one answer to what to plant in such places. It does very well on chalk and is a good plant for seaside gardens as it stands up well to searing winds and salt spray.

It is not very elegant as far as habit is concerned, especially if pruning is neglected, for then it will grow nearly 10 feet tall, but look leggy and straggly. Hard pruning in March will help and the more straggly shoots can be cut hard back and the other shoots reduced in length. Even so, after a few years, plants will inevitably become leggy. To prevent this spoiling the effect it pays to plant a lower-growing shrub or a clump of herbaceous perennials in front of the Spanish Broom.

Planting out, as this shrub does not like root disturbance, should be done from pot plants. Transplanting from the open ground should only be done if absolutely essential as it usually kills the plant.

Spartium junceum will not make an elegant shrub if allowed to grow freely. It should be hard pruned in March.

Spiraea

This is another biggish group of shrubs, with about fifty kinds available, though for the normal shrub garden the selection can be limited to a few. Even these are varied in height, habit and flower colour.

The most familiar kind is the hybrid *S.* × *arguta,* known to many gardeners as the Bridal Wreath, a shrub eventually about 6 feet tall, with slender arching stems, wreathed in April and May with multitudes of tiny white flowers. To ensure that the shrub has ample opportunity to produce the long new shoots on which the flowers appear, it is necessary to prune after flowering at about the end of May, cutting back hard the old stems that have flowered.

The equally popular *S.* × *bumalda* 'Anthony Waterer' must be treated even more drastically for in April it should be cut practically down to the ground. It will then produce masses of stems, about 2 feet tall, which, in late summer will bear flattish heads of crimson flowers. If these are cut off after they have faded, more may be produced well into September. Those who like variegated foliage should note that very often the leaves of this shrub are variegated with pink and creamy-white.

S. thunbergii starts the season by flowering in late March

Spiraea × *arguta* is the hybrid shrub known as the Bridal Wreath.

or early April. In habit and in flower it is not unlike *S.* × *arguta,* but it is not so tall, reaching 4 feet. It should be pruned in the same way.

S. × *vanhouttei,* again similar in habit and flower to *S.* × *arguta,* flowers in June, but is taller, growing to about 7–8 feet.

All these spiraeas, flowering as they do on new growth, benefit from reasonably generous treatment and annual pruning. They have no particular soil requirements but do better if the soil is well dug and enriched with compost at planting time and if it is given an annual mulch of compost, rotted manure or hop manure.

The hybrid *S.* × *bumalda* has crimson flowers and variegated foliage.

Syringa yunnanensis

Syringa

The syringas are the lilacs, not the philadelphus, as explained elsewhere. They have long been popular for their fragrant flowers, appearing from about the middle of May to early June, but although this is a short flowering period few gardeners would wish to omit lilacs from their gardens.

The ordinary lilac, *S. vulgaris,* with its mauve flowers, is a good shrub, but there are finer kinds, developed from it over the past sixty years or so. Because lilacs are easy to grow they are apt to be neglected and allowed to look after themselves, so that all too often they do not give of their best. The trouble is, perhaps, that they will literally grow almost anywhere, in sunny places, no matter what type of soil they have to put up with. They will do much better, however, if they are mulched annually with well-rotted compost or a general fertilizer, although this should not be dug in but spread around, to be absorbed gradually into the soil. The shrubs will flower better if time can be found to cut off dead flower-heads and to remove sucker growths.

Among the most magnificent kinds are the double-flowered varieties such as 'Katherine Havemeyer', deep lavender-purple, 'Madame A. Buchner', pinkish-mauve, 'Mrs Edward Harding', rosy-carmine, and 'Souvenir de Alice Harding', white. All these have large fragrant flowers in large trusses.

Good single-flowered varieties include 'Clarke's Giant', 'Marchal Foch', and 'Primrose'.

The double forms of the ordinary lilac, *Syringa vulgaris,* produce magnificent displays.

Viburnum

There are about seventy-five viburnums in cultivation but most of these are little known. Some of the more popular kinds are evergreen, others deciduous, some are grown for their flowers, some for their fruit. A few add brilliant autumn leaf colour to their other attributes.

The winter-flowering kinds are good value as they bloom at a time when flower-interest is at a premium. The old *V. tinus*, commonly known as Laurustinus, is widely planted, usually as a specimen, although it makes a good evergreen hedge. Its heads of white flowers begin to appear in Novem-

Viburnum davidii

ber and it is early spring before flowering ceases. *V.* × *burkwoodii,* an evergreen hybrid, with fragrant white flowers that open from early in the New Year to early spring, is outstanding. It is followed into flower by *V. carlesii,* a deciduous species with clusters of fragrant white flowers. One of the most striking of the spring-flowering kinds is *V. rhitidophyllum*, an evergreen, 10 feet or more tall, with large leaves, white below, and large clusters of white flowers.

This, however, is not as fine as *V. tomentosum* in its forms 'Lanarth' or *mariesii*. This is a leaf-losing shrub, eventually about 6 feet tall, its branches held out horizontally. Along these in May and June appear flat heads of white flowers not unlike those of some hydrangeas in that the inner, fertile ones are surrounded by larger sterile flowers. The leaves of this viburnum are briefly magnificent in autumn when they turn crimson.

The leaves of our native Guelder Rose, *V. opulus,* also colour well in autumn and add to the value of the shrub for its white flowers in May and June and its clusters of red fruits in autumn. Old specimens may reach 15 feet.

Worth growing for its fruit alone is the dwarf evergreen species, *V. davidii,* about 2 feet tall, with bright blue berries on female plants. Both male and female types must be planted to ensure fruiting.

All these are easy shrubs to grow, and do well on chalky soils. Normal ground preparation is sufficient and no pruning is needed unless it is to remove dead wood. All are hardy. *V. davidii* is a good kind to grow in groups.

V. opulus sterile and
V. fragrans (*right*)

Species of *Parthenocissus* are excellent for covering house walls.

Vitis

These are the Vines and vine relatives, the Virginia Creepers and similar plants that, for the sake of convenience, the closely related genera *Ampelopsis* and *Parthenocissus* are included under this heading, particularly as from the gardener's point of view there is little to differentiate them. Those grown in British gardens are all deciduous climbers, some of them self-clinging by means of small 'sucker-pads', others needing support. Most of them are notable for their brilliant autumn foliage tints, a few produce bunches of grape-like fruits following their greenish, insignificant flowers. They are usually seen clothing walls, and many of them are excellent on north or east walls, but they are also good plants for fences, pergolas, archways, tree stumps or for growing into trees. Like wisterias, they may be used to smother outhouses, sheds, garages and the like, without doing structural damage to the buildings.

None of these useful climbers is fussy about soil, but, like any climber planted near a wall, it is worth enriching the soil before planting, since these sites are usually poor and dry

Vitis coignetiae covers the arch. (*Above*) a leaf of *Parthenocissus quinquefolia*.

and overhanging eaves may keep them dry, even in wet weather. Compost, moist peat or leafmould dug into the soil in generous quantities, with the site widely and deeply dug, should ensure that the plants get a good start and will continue to make rapid growth. No pruning is needed.

The most striking plant for shady walls is *Parthenocissus* (*Vitis*) *henryana,* a tendril climber, with delightful purple and white variegated leaves that turn red in autumn. The true Virginia Creeper is *Parthenocissus* (*Vitis*) *quinquefolia,* with bright scarlet and orange leaves in autumn. The popular large-leaved 'Virginia Creeper' is *P. tricuspidata,* the leaves of which turn the most fiery colours in October. Of the true Ampelopsis, *A. brevipeduculata* is the best because not only do its hop-like leaves colour well but it also has bunches of china-blue grapes in autumn.

Another striking plant is *Vitis coignetiae,* with leaves up to 1 foot across, turning to all imaginable shades of crimson and orange in autumn. This is better for a pergola, or for covering an outhouse, rather than for a wall.

The garden varieties (*above*)
are derived from *W. florida.*

Weigela

The weigelas, still sometimes catalogued as diervillas, are among those shrubs that give their best if they are properly pruned, the old, flowered shoots cut back hard to encourage the production of new flowering growth. However, they are easy shrubs to grow and even if pruning is neglected they still put up a reasonably good show.

They will grow well in any normal garden soil, including those that contain much chalk or lime. They will survive in exposed, wind-swept positions, but, to look their best they should be given ample space, for, although they do not grow more than 5–6 feet tall, their arching growths cover an area of about 6 feet in diameter.

Weigela florida, the commonest kind, has rosy-pink flowers in May and early June, sometimes followed by a later flush, but there are better and brighter hybrids. Among these 'Newport Red', the crimson 'Eva Rathke', the white 'Mont Blanc' and the large-flowered pink 'Conquete' are among the best.

Weigela florida variegata adds leaf variegation to its attraction and is among the best of variegated leaf shrubs, slower-growing than the type, but a constant pleasure from spring to autumn, with its leaves broadly edged with white. The purple-leaved form, *foliis purpureis,* has its own attraction. Both varieties have pink flowers.

Weigela florida variegata

Wisteria

Wisterias are very vigorous climbing shrubs, most useful for covering walls, pergolas, fences and the like, and even capable of smothering garages and other out-buildings beneath their growths, or growing up into trees. However, by careful attention to pruning, they can be kept within reasonable bounds and it is, in fact, possible to train them as standard trees, their long growths weeping down to the ground. Pruning is done in autumn or winter, when the plants are gone over to see which shoots are to be retained to extend the growth. The remainder are then cut back to within about 3 inches of the point at which they spring from the older shoots. Longer shoots retained for extension purposes may be tipped and, to restrict growth further, all shoots may be lightly pruned in August. But, where plants are grown over trees no pruning is needed.

W. sinensis is the species usually grown. It has a white variety, *alba,* and one with double flowers, *plena.*

Wisterias are not particularly fussy about the soil in which they are grown, but the planting site should be well prepared, deeply and widely dug, with ample quantities of well-rotted compost or leafmould incorporated.

Wisteria sinensis has foot long trails of fragrant mauve flowers.

SPECIAL PURPOSE SHRUBS

* The inclusion of a particular shrub in this list does not mean that it will not grow in more open, sunny positions. In any case, few shrubs will grow in deep shade.

FOR SHADE*

Berberis darwinii
Berberis × stenophylla
Camellias
Choisya ternata
Cornus kousa
Cotoneaster simonsii
Daphne mezereum
Forsythia spectabilis
Hydrangea macrophylla
Hydrangea paniculata
Hypericum calycinum
Kerria japonica
Olearia haastii
Prunus laurocerasus
Prunus lusitanicus
Pyracanthas
Rhododendron (Azalea)
  Kurume Hybrids
  Mollis Hybrids
Ribes sanguineum
Viburnum tinus

FOR CHALKY SOILS

Berberis
Buddleias
Caryopteris
Cercis
Chaenomeles
Choisya ternata
Cistus
Clematis
Clerodendrum
Cornus
Cotoneasters
Crataegus
Cytisus
Daphne mezereum
Deutzias

Erica carnea
Forsythias
Fuchsias
Garrya elliptica
Genistas
Hebe
Helianthemums
Hibiscus
Hypericums
Laburnum
Lavandulas
Loniceras
Malus
Philadelphus
Potentillas
Prunus
Rhus
Ribes
Rosa
Senecio
Sorbus
Spartium
Spiraea
Syringa
Vibusnum
Weigela

FOR DRY SOILS AND SUNNY SITES

Acer
Berberis
Calluna
Caryopteris
Chaenomeles
Cistus
Cotoneasters
Cytisus
Ericas
Genistas
Hebes
Helianthemums
Hypericums
Lavandulas
Olearias
Potentillas
Rhus
Senecio,
Spartium
Spiraea

FOR TOWN GARDENS

Amelanchiers
Berberis
Caryopteris
Chaenomeles
Cornus
Cotoneasters
Cytisus
Deutzias
Forsythias
Hibiscus
Hypericums
Jasminums
Kerrias
Laburnums
Malus
Olearias
Philadelphus
Prunus
Pyracanthas
Rhododendrons
Rhus
Ribes
Senecio
Sorbus
Spiraea
Syringa
Viburnum
Weigela

MONTHS AND SEASONS

The months and seasons mentioned in this book apply to temperate regions of the northern hemisphere (Europe, Canada and the northern United States). For readers living in other regions, the following table gives approximate equivalents.

Subtropical regions of the northern hemisphere (*Mediterranean sea, southern United States*)

Plants will tend to shoot and flower a month or so earlier in these regions.

Tropical regions (*around the equator*)

No seasons exist in the tropical regions. There are no set times for planting, and the suitability of growing an individual plant will depend on local climatic conditions.

Subtropical regions of the southern hemisphere (*Australasia, South America, southern Africa*)

The seasons are reversed in these regions. Spring is approximately from September to November, summer from December to February, autumn from March to May, and winter from June to August.

INDEX

Page numbers in bold type refer to illustrations.